END TIMES,
THE MIDDLE EAST, AND
THE NEW WORLD ORDER

END TIMES,
THE MIDDLE EAST, AND

THE NEW
WORLD
ORDER

ED HINDSON

VICTOR BOOKS ®

A DIVISION OF SCRIPTURE PRESS PUBLICATIONS INC.
USA CANADA ENGLAND

The author expresses appreciation to Phyllis Janish for typing the original manuscript.

Unless otherwise indicated, all Scripture references are from the *Holy Bible, New International Version,* © 1973, 1978, 1984, International Bible Society. Used by permission of Zondervan Bible Publishers; other Scripture quotations are from the *Authorized (King James) Version* (KJV).

Cover illustration by B.E. Johnson © 1991

Library of Congress Cataloging-in-Publication Data
Hindson, Edward E.
    End times, the Middle East, and the new world order / by Ed Hindson.
      p.   cm.
    ISBN 0-89693-951-0
    1. Bible—Prophecies.   I. Title.
BS647.2.H55   1991
220.1'5—dc20   91-17535
                                              CIP

---

1 2 3 4 5 6 7 8 9 10 Printing/Year 95 94 93 92 91

CONTENTS

Preface / *7*

1. What in the World Is Happening? / *11*
War in the Middle East! Iraq invades Kuwait. Saddam Hussein proclaims himself the new Nebuchadnezzar and calls for a holy war against Israel. Biblical prophecy unfolds before our eyes.

2. The March to Armageddon / *29*
Just when peace and a new world order seemed so promising, Iraq upset the balance. Less than a year after the collapse of communism in Eastern Europe and the end of the Cold War, the world was at war.

3. The End Is Near . . . Or Is It? / *49*
Jesus Christ predicted wars, famines, earthquakes, and persecution as well as the signs of the end of the age, but He also warned us not to set any dates.

4. Miscalculating the Second Coming / *65*
Many have proposed dates for the Second Coming and candidates for the Antichrist—without success.

5. The Gathering Storm / 86
The threat of nuclear destruction and a great Islamic *jihad*, "holy war," against Israel are now appearing on the horizon. Time may be running out for a lasting peace.

6. The New World Order / 111
A unified Europe may achieve economic and political leadership of the new world order.

7. Can There Be Lasting Peace in the Middle East? / 126
Peace treaties have been tried before, but always without lasting success. Is the stage now set for the rise of a world peacemaker and the treaty to end all treaties?

8. Prophecies of the End Times / 140
Biblical prophecies warn of a Great Tribulation coming. The key players are clearly predicted by name.

9. What Is Next? / 157
The Bible predicts a spiritual apostasy in the last days. It also predicts the Rapture of the church, the Great Tribulation, the Battle of Armageddon, the return of Christ, His millennial reign on earth, and finally, the new heaven and new earth.

10. It Isn't Over Till It's Over / 172
The Bible gives five specific indications of when the end will come. In the meantime, believers are given specific tasks to fulfill.

Notes / 185

Maps / 201

PREFACE

The recent Gulf War was the most televised and publicized war ever. Live reports via satellite brought the dramatic events of the war right inside our homes. Most of us sat on the edge of our seats as we strained to catch every detail of SCUD missile attacks, air raid warnings, nighttime infrared television bombs, and even a tank war viewed from ground level on the sands of the Middle East.

We could not help but be captivated by the incredible details of the conflict rapidly unfolding before our eyes. It was the greatest television event of all time—a live war from the Middle East! We were instantly transported from Jerusalem to Baghdad to Riyadh to Amman to Tel Aviv. In many ways, the Gulf War was a microcosm of the great end-times conflict known as the Battle of Armageddon.

Every time there is a war in the Middle East, students of biblical prophecy get excited. They realize that this could be the Big One. But one of the dangers of such expectation is that it easily leads to uncontrolled speculation—often premature and sometimes even misleading.

The purpose of this book is to examine the legitimacy of Bible prophecy while critiquing the excessive speculation of well-meaning, but nonbiblical, attempts to predict the future. My tone will not be harsh because I believe that most evangelicals are genuinely concerned about prophetic events and sincerely anticipate the coming of Christ.

It is my sincere hope that all of my readers, regardless of their eschatology, will benefit from the words of caution that I raise. It is also my profound desire that the information in this book and the spirit in which it is written will increase your interest in the serious study of biblical prophecy. Jesus Christ Himself said: "Behold, I am coming soon! Blessed is he who keeps the words of the prophecy in this book" (Revelation 22:7).

Ed Hindson

END TIMES, THE MIDDLE EAST, AND THE NEW WORLD ORDER

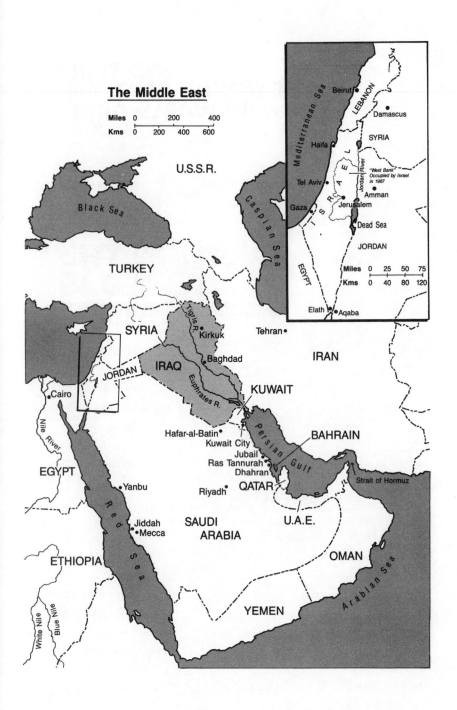

The Middle East

Miles 0 ___ 200 ___ 400
Kms 0 _ 200 _ 400 _ 600

U.S.S.R.

Black Sea

Caspian Sea

TURKEY

SYRIA

Tigris R.

Kirkuk

Baghdad

IRAQ

Euphrates R.

JORDAN

Cairo

Nile River

EGYPT

Tehran

IRAN

KUWAIT

Hafar-al-Batin
Kuwait City
Jubail
Ras Tannurah
Dhahran

Persian Gulf

BAHRAIN

QATAR

Strait of Hormuz

U.A.E.

Riyadh

Yanbu

Red Sea

Jiddah
Mecca

SAUDI
ARABIA

OMAN

ETHIOPIA

Arabian Sea

White Nile

Blue Nile

YEMEN

Inset map

Mediterranean Sea

Beirut

LEBANON

Damascus

SYRIA

Haifa

I S R A E L

Tel Aviv

"West Bank"
Occupied by Israel
in 1967

Jordan River

Gaza

Jerusalem

Amman

Dead Sea

EGYPT

JORDAN

Miles 0 _ 25 _ 50 _ 75
Kms 0 _ 40 _ 80 _ 120

Elath

Aqaba

1

WHAT IN THE WORLD IS HAPPENING?

The chill night wind whirled about me as I raced across the parking lot to my car. The winter darkness was quickly evaporating the dismal sunset as I reached for my keys. Balancing books and trying to find the keyhole is an acrobatic stunt every teacher learns to perform.

"Wait!" shouted a female voice. "We want to ask you a question," one of my students hollered out, tugging at her boyfriend to follow along.

"Sure, what is it?" I responded, trying to use my car door as a shield against the wind.

"We were just wondering about everything that's happening in the Middle East," she continued. "Do you think this could be the end of the world?" she asked intently.

"I suppose it could be," I replied, "but that doesn't mean it will be. Possibility and probability aren't necessarily the same thing."

"What do you mean?" she asked, looking somewhat bewildered.

"Let me put it this way," I suggested. "Just because it is

possible that something *could* happen doesn't mean it is probable, or likely, that it *will* happen."

We talked about the Middle East crisis and its prophetic implications. Finally, her boyfriend said, "Well, I guess we should go ahead and study tonight!"

"Yes!" I said. "Whatever you do, don't drop out of school!"

WAR IN THE MIDDLE EAST

January 15, 1991 will always remain indelibly etched in our minds. For 166 days, from Iraq's invasion of Kuwait on August 2, 1990, until the deadline set by the United Nations Security Council, the world waited in fearful anticipation of war in the Middle East. Just when lasting peace had seemed such a real possibility, Saddam Hussein upset the plans for a new world order.

"It all sounds like the replay of some ancient biblical drama," a friend told me. Then, reflecting for a moment, he wondered if it might not have *prophetic* significance. "Isn't Iraq ancient Babylon?" Tom asked. "Do you suppose this could lead to something like Armageddon?"

Questions like these began to grip the hearts of believers and nonbelievers alike. "Iraqiphobia" spread like a plague. Fears of poison gas attacks, chemical and biological warfare, and even nuclear destruction reminded the world that its frail attempts at a lasting peace are limited by human depravity—greed and the lust for power.

The vulnerability of our own lives is always challenged in a time of war. We are forced to look more deeply at the basic issues and ultimate realities of life. Despite the beauty of this earth and the affluent quality of our lives, war shockingly reminds us that this life is still a "vale of tears." Our real destiny is in the dust, and somehow a world without God knew it and sensed it quickly as war engulfed the media.

Soon the newspapers of the world began screaming their headlines: "Geneva Peace Talks Fail" (January 10); "War in the Middle East" (January 16); "U.S. Bombs Baghdad" (January 17); "Israel Hit by Missiles" (January 18). Satellite-relayed telecasts gave us each a front-row seat for the greatest television drama ever—a live war in the Middle East.

War in the Middle East! Israel under attack! It sounded all too familiar to those of us raised on Bible prophecy. "Could this really be Armageddon?" some wondered.

"I can't believe this is actually happening right before my eyes!" a friend exclaimed.

"Things are happening so fast that I bet even Hal Lindsey[1] is confused!" a pastor told me with a gleam in his eye.

Others wondered what all the talk about a "new world order" meant. "It sounds to me like we've come down to the end and it's about all over," a Sunday School teacher suggested to me. "The Antichrist is almost certainly alive— biding his time, awaiting his cue," one well-known Bible teacher exclaimed.[2]

After 40 days of Allied bombing in over 100,000 sorties, the ground war finally began. To the world's surprise, it was all over in 100 hours! The greatest tank war since World War II left 90 percent of Iraq's tanks captured or destroyed. Nearly 100,000 Iraqi soldiers surrendered to the Allies, many of them at the point of starvation and devastation. Rather than the final battle, Desert Storm was a microcosm of Armageddon yet to come.

VISION OF A NEW WORLD ORDER

The vision of a better world has often propelled great leaders to predict peace and prosperity based on a plan to restructure the way in which people and nations relate to one another. Ironically, Mikhail Gorbachev of the Soviet Union was the first world leader to publicly suggest the need for a "new world order" in his address to the United Nations on December 7, 1988. In what may well have been a prophetic insight, the Soviet leader said, "Further global progress is now possible only through a quest for universal consensus in the movement towards a new world order."[3]

In the events that followed that historic address, the world watched with amazement, anticipation, and at times, nearly numbed disbelief as the communist regimes of Eastern Europe began to collapse like a row of dominoes. As the Berlin Wall was torn down and the throngs of thousands shouting, "Democracy!" filled the public squares of Europe's formerly communist strongholds, it truly did seem that a new world order was emerging.

Newspapers around the world pronounced the end of the Cold War between the United States and the Soviet Union. Everyone was talking about the coming world peace—*Pax Americana*. President George Bush, following Gorbachev's lead, also began talking about a new world order with the United Nations as the chief cornerstone for world peace.

At the opening of NATO at Turnbury, Scotland in June 1990, President Bush announced that a "new European order" was emerging after the collapse of communism in Eastern Europe. The world certainly appeared to offer every prospect of peace, security, and stability for the future. The Berlin Wall was down, democracy was sweeping the nations of formerly communist Europe, Germany was reunited, and the Cold War was officially over.

Hope for unprecedented world cooperation was running high as Saddam Hussein mobilized his army along the border of Iraq and Kuwait in midsummer. Catching the world by total surprise, except for the Israelis who had been protesting for months, Hussein suddenly posed the greatest threat to peace in the post-Cold War era.

Despite the Iraqi threat, President Bush expressed hope for "the foundation of the new world order" to be laid out in his September summit meeting with Gorbachev at Helsinki, Finland. Optimism was still running high on September 10, 1990 when Secretary of State James Baker declared on "Face the Nation" that we are "on the verge of forming a new world order." Addressing the United Nations a few days later, on September 25, 1990, Soviet Foreign Minister Eduard Shevardnadze denounced Iraq as a "threat to the new world order."[4]

TEN THOUSAND FEET BELOW THE DESERT

At the heart of Iraq's dispute with Kuwait was the huge, fifty-mile long, banana-shaped Rumaila oil field, which straddles the Iraq-Kuwait border. Ten thousand feet below the desert floor lies one of the world's largest and richest oil reserves. Though most of the oil field lies under Iraq, oil can be pumped out by the Kuwaitis at the other end. In Saddam Hussein's mind, Kuwait has been stealing his oil and he wants it back. Likewise, the U.S.A. would object strongly if Canada decided to drain one of the Great Lakes along our common border.

Usually participants in a shared oil field divide the production costs and revenue based on percentage of ownership. But Iraq refused to negotiate with Kuwait on such an agreement, so the Kuwaitis went ahead and pumped alone. In the meantime, Kuwait exceeded the quota system established by the Organization of Petroleum Exporting Countries (OPEC) and its overproduction pushed down the price of oil and revenue for all OPEC members.

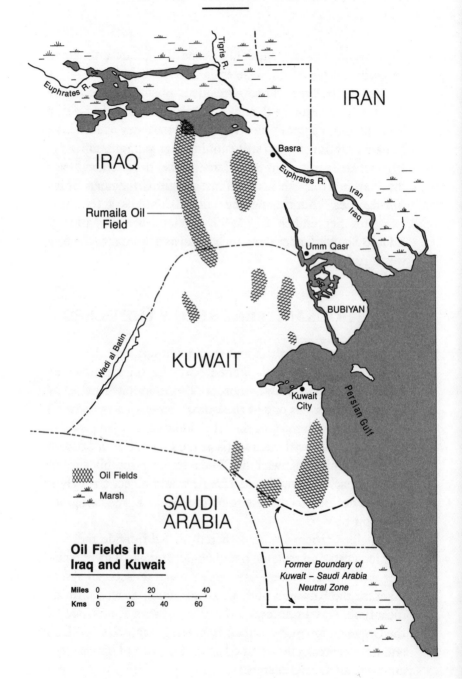

IRAN

Tigris R.

Euphrates R.

IRAQ

Basra

Euphrates R.

Iran
Iraq

Rumaila Oil
Field

Umm Qasr

BUBIYAN

Wadi al Batin

KUWAIT

Kuwait
City

Persian Gulf

Oil Fields

Marsh

SAUDI
ARABIA

**Oil Fields in
Iraq and Kuwait**

Former Boundary of
*Kuwait – Saudi Arabia
Neutral Zone*

Miles	0		20		40
Kms	0	20	40	60	

For many this argument over oil is at the heart of the current crisis in the Middle East. Hussein's decision to invade Kuwait on August 2, 1990 was his response to settling this dispute. However, some Middle East experts claim this is an excuse to cover up Iraq's long-held desire to plunder Kuwait's wealth and to control its 200-mile-long coastline on the Persian Gulf.

"The issue of oil taken from the Rumaila field is only a smokescreen to disguise Iraq's more ambitious intentions," claims Marvin Zonis, economics professor at The University of Chicago. "The Iraqis will claim anything to justify the incorporation of Kuwait."[5]

Iraq's dispute over Kuwait goes all the way back to Britain's decision in 1899 to establish Kuwait as a British protectorate under the Emir of Kuwait. The Emir's family had ruled the area since 1756, but Iraq still considered it part of its southern province.

The dispute flared again when oil was discovered in the Rumaila reservoir in Iraq in 1953. It took the intervention of both the Arab League and British military forces to settle the issue then, but the antagonism has remained ever since. "Saddam Hussein's kind of aggression has to be answered," *Fortune* magazine declared, "because oil is the most vital ingredient of the modern economy."[6] Whoever controls the world's oil fields controls the world.

A LINE IN THE SAND

The blitz of Kuwait on August 2, 1990 by Iraq's combat-hardened troops and tank convoys overthrew the tiny nation and sent its royal family scurrying into exile. Saddam Hussein had taken the biggest gamble of his military career and refused to withdraw. Intelligence reports convinced U.S.

President George Bush that Hussein fully intended to bring Saudi Arabia under his control as well, leaving himself as the oil kingpin over 62 percent of the world's oil reserves. Such a position would have enabled Hussein to tip the world's balance of power in whatever direction he wanted.

World reaction to Hussein's virtual rape of Kuwait came quickly and decisively. At Saudi Arabia's request the United States immediately sent thousands of troops to secure the Saudi-Kuwait border and halt any further aggression by Iraq. The Security Council of the United Nations passed twelve resolutions against Iraq demanding immediate withdrawal and the restoration of Kuwait's legitimate government. Bush met Soviet President Mikhail Gorbachev at Helsinki, Finland, in September 1990, and they issued a joint statement calling on Iraq to "withdraw unconditionally" from Kuwait. Bush then began building a twenty-eight-nation multinational coalition against Iraq in the most massive military buildup since the Vietnam War.

By late November 1990, the United Nations Security Council voted 12-2, with China abstaining, to authorize force to liberate Kuwait and set January 15, 1991, as the date by which Iraq must withdraw or face punitive action. For the first time since the Korean War, forty-five years earlier, the UN had authorized military action against an aggressor nation.

In reaction to the United Nations sanctions and demands, Saddam Hussein refused to negotiate or withdraw and called for an Arab Holy War (*jihad*) against the demons from the West. George Bush had drawn "a line in the sand" at the Saudi border and warned Iraq that its aggression would not be rewarded. When last-minute efforts for a resolution were rebuffed by Iraqi Foreign Minister Tariq Aziz at Geneva, Switzerland on January 9, 1991, the stage was set for war in the Middle East.

"THE MOTHER OF ALL BATTLES"

Saddam Hussein, the father of all rhetoric, warned the Western powers that the "Mother of All Battles" was about to begin. Like many Muslim leaders, he began to salt his political speeches with religious terms while appealing to three major Arab themes: poverty, piety, and the Palestinians. He denounced the Kuwaitis for their wanton wealth, proclaimed George Bush the Great Satan, demanded the reinstatement of the Palestinian State, and called for a holy war against the United Nations coalition demanding his withdrawal from occupied Kuwait. In a final gesture of twisted piety, Saddam ordained that *Allahu Akbar* (God is Great) be sewed into the Iraqi flag.

In the strange metaphysics of war, Hussein has become a master of disguises, erupting forth in a dozen moral charades. Always attempting to use the media to his advantage, he often miscalculated public response. The raids on Israel provoked international outrage, as did his parade of battered American POWs and the ecological disaster of the great oil spill in the Persian Gulf. Finally, in the face of certain defeat he said, "If this is martyrdom, let it come . . . the alternative is humiliation!"

The absence of accountability in a dictatorship often allows a leader like Saddam "to escape reality on the horse of rhetoric," as one fellow Arab described it.[7] Words often create and then manipulate the truth, and Hussein gambled that he could intimidate the world into backing down with his resolve to stand firm on Kuwait.

For many Arabs, Saddam represents their yearnings for dignity, unity, and honor. He also symbolizes their resistance to foreign domination and their desire for a more equitable distribution of Arab oil wealth. Hussein's Baath (renaissance) Party appeals to Arab hopes for a better world of their own. Such hopes often allow his followers to overlook his despotism and reign of terror at home.

THE NEW NEBUCHADNEZZAR

The suffering of the Iraqi people and the destruction of Iraq are mere consequences of Hussein's personal pride and ambition. Following the example of his patron hero Gamal Abdel Nasser of Egypt, who stood up against the West and attacked Israel in 1956, Saddam sees himself as a kind of modern-day Nebuchadnezzar, the ancient king of Babylon who destroyed Jerusalem and led Israel into the Babylonian Captivity in the sixth century B.C.

During the war with Iran (1980–1988), Saddam even began a rebuilding project at the archeological site of ancient Babylon. By 1987 Hussein's "Disneyland in the Desert" was being heavily financed as a symbol of national pride and a link to the past. Hussein even sponsored an international festival at Babylon in 1987 whose official seal contained a side-by-side look-alike of Hussein and Nebuchadnezzar.[8]

Hussein was born in 1937 into an illiterate peasant family in a small village on the edge of the northern Iraqi town of Tikrit on the banks of the Tigris River. Ironically, this is the same town that birthed Saladin, the great Muslim warrior of the twelfth century A.D. He too rose from the obscurity of this hardscrabble village to lead the Muslims in a holy war against the West. Saladin captured Jerusalem in 1187, which led to the Third Crusade.

Saddam Hussein is a madman by Western standards, but he is not crazy by any standards. He is cold, ruthless, and calculating—reflecting the passions and complexities of the Arab world. Raised by an abusive stepfather and an angry pro-Nazi uncle, he learned to hate foreigners as intruders in the Muslim "Holy Land." As a student in the 1950s, Saddam was captivated by the Arab nationalism sweeping the region and Nasser of Egypt became his personal hero.[9]

At age twenty Saddam joined the secular and somewhat socialist Baath Party. Within two years he attempted to assassinate Iraq's military strongman Abdul Kassem and barely escaped with his life. But his basic personality and style of leadership was already becoming clear. In 1958 he murdered his own brother-in-law because he was a Kassem supporter. After a period of exile in Cairo, Egypt, Hussein returned to Iraq in 1963 and began his rise to power as a ruthless tyrant. He organized the secret police, used torture to inflict punishment, and eventually became the chairman of the Revolutionary Command Council under President Ahmad Hassan al-Bakr in 1968.

JONESTOWN REVISITED

Saddam, whose name means "he who confronts," became President of Iraq in 1979, when Bakr handed over the leadership of the nation to him. Hussein immediately began a ruthless purge to eliminate all who would not bow to his power and authority. He videotaped a public "confession" of a member of the Command Council who implicated himself and four colleagues in a plot against Saddam. Hussein then ordered the other party members to execute them in a mass firing squad. Some accounts claim that as many as 500 Baathists were executed in the summer of 1979.[10]

Other accounts tell of a party official who dared to disagree with Saddam and was condemned to die. When the official's wife pled with Hussein to return her husband to her, he assured her that he would—then had him chopped into pieces, dumped into a bag, and sent to her house!

Hussein's internal reign of terror consolidated his personal power to such an extent that no one dared oppose him. *Time* magazine noted, "In Saddam's world, falsehood was often propelled by fear. . . . Saddam's aides sometimes withhold critical information about the war from him because they are afraid of telling him the truth."[11] Dan Rather, CBS anchorman, traveled to Baghdad in the fall of 1990 and conducted a personal interview with Hussein. Later, Rather explained that Saddam's staff appeared rational and congenial when Rather was alone with them, but when Hussein entered the room, everything changed and they jumped to fulfill his every wish.

Some have likened Saddam's hypnotic appeal and reign of terror to Jim Jones and his infamous People's Temple cult at Jonestown, Guyana—only on a very much larger scale. A recent article in *Time* magazine suggests: "There is in Baghdad a feeling of a huge new Jonestown, with another demented preacher leading his flock to death."[12]

The Iraqis have found themselves isolated from the real world, led by a paranoid government of men who shot their way to power and imagine everyone as their enemy. Tragically, tens of thousands of Iraqis were sacrificed in a deathtrap to keep their leader's delusions alive. And Iraqi money which could have helped rebuild the country has been squandered on Hussein's self-glorification.

GEORGE BUSH AND "THE LAST CRUSADE"

The ruthless marriage of Iraqi ambition and Western technology set the stage for a last great crusade against Muslim expansionism. But this crusade found Arabs on both sides of the conflict. Brother was set against brother in the greatest threat to Arab unity yet to crack the Muslim hegemony over the desert sands.

The United Nations mandate for the withdrawal of Iraq from Kuwait by January 15, 1991 divided the Arab world, leaving some leaders hopelessly caught in the middle between national diplomacy and popular sentiment. The expulsion of the often hated Kuwaitis and Hussein's threats against Israel brought a surge of Arab patriotism and nationalism throughout the Muslim world.

The United States, with Arab cooperation, led a twenty-eight-nation multinational force into Saudi Arabia to set up a line of defense against Iraq, called the "Desert Shield." For the first time since the British battled the Turks in the early twentieth century, Western armies were standing on Muslim holy ground poised for a great crusade. The Desert Shield was about to become the Desert Storm.

"I've got it boiled down very clearly to good versus evil," President Bush announced to the National Religious Broadcasters Convention in Washington, D.C. just a week after the war had begun. The President was convinced that Hussein must be punished for his aggression or it would only encourage more aggression as did the initial appeasement of Hitler prior to World War II.

On January 16, 1991, George Bush faced the nation in the most watched event in television history and announced, "Tonight the battle has been joined . . . and we will win!" In that address he also added, "We have before us the opportunity to forge for ourselves and for future generations a new world order, where the rule of law, not the law of the jungle, governs the conduct of nations." A few weeks later on March 6, 1991, President Bush addressed the joint houses of Congress with his triumphant victory speech. On that night he announced: "Our success in the Gulf will shape the new world order we seek."

LIVE FROM THE MIDDLE EAST

The eyes of the world were riveted on the first war of the age of global information. It all began right in the middle of the U.S. TV networks' evening newscasts and held the world spellbound over the next several days. Various American reporters provided an unprecedented live account of the war from inside the enemy capital. As the bombs burst overhead, ABC correspondent Gary Shepard in Baghdad announced, "An attack is under way." So was the greatest television drama of all time.

Three CNN reporters on the ninth floor of the Al Rashid Hotel, Bernard Shaw, Peter Arnett, and John Holliman provided a live account of the start of the war which reminded older generations of Edward R. Murrow's live radio broadcasts from London during the Nazi blitz. "Something is happening outside . . . we're getting star bursts in the black sky," Shaw reported.

"They're coming over our hotel. You can hear the bombs now," Arnett announced to the stunned world.

"This feels like the center of hell," Shaw added.

Meanwhile, the television networks cancelled all regular programming and provided continuous coverage for the next forty-two hours. President Bush's speech on Wednesday night, January 16, drew the biggest audience in television history—61 million households. Then the bombardment of information began. The public was deluged with information about the war. In the next several hours, we learned about SCUD missiles, Tomahawks, Patriots, mobile-launchers, cruise missiles, surgical bombing, carpet bombing, F-15s, M1s, cluster bombs, laser-range finders, smart bombs, and even the TOW 2 (*T*ube-launched *O*ptically tracked *W*ire-guided) anti-tank missile. We were given live reports by military experts, retired generals, political analysts, Middle East experts, world leaders, local politicians, and eyewitnesses.

Then, in what *Time* magazine called "another quirk of timing oddly fitted for the TV age, the drama often heated up just as the prime-time hours approached."[13] On Thursday night viewers watched with nervous apprehension as correspondents in Jerusalem and Tel Aviv relayed reports of Iraqi missiles hitting Israel. NBC's Martin Fletcher in Tel Aviv conducted his live report while wearing a gas mask as precaution against a possible chemical attack.

These images will long remain in our minds. Like the John F. Kennedy assassination or the space shuttle explosion, their impact transcended every other thing happening in our lives at that moment. Most of us will never forget where we were or what we were doing when it all began. I had just finished a four-night Bible study series at a church in St. Louis. We cut short the last night so we could all gather around a television set in the parlor to watch the President's speech. It was an incredible moment as the seriousness of the specter that lay ahead gripped us all.

AN EYE ON PROPHECY

The unprovoked Iraqi attack on Israel angered the civilized world. Emotional support for the Jewish nation rose immediately and dramatically. Iraq's indiscriminate launching of its "to whom it may concern" Scud missiles arbitrarily blasted Tel Aviv's civilian neighborhoods, bringing havoc and destruction. For those familiar with biblical prophecies, even greater images were flashing through their minds. "Could this be the Battle of Gog and Magog or even Armageddon?" one stunned housewife asked as we stared ominously at the television report.

There can be little doubt that the Bible predicts a great conflict between Israel and her Arab neighbors in the "last days" (Ezekiel 38:8, 16). Even among the Arabs there is an ancient popular, but apocryphal, tale that predicts the Bedouin of Arabia, allied with the Franks (Europeans) and Egypt will gather in the desert against a man called Sadam [sic] and they will all be killed and none will escape. Many Arabs believe the text predicts the destruction of the enemies of Saddam Hussein.[14]

Others, including Ahmad Oweidi Abbadi, chairman of the Jordanian National Front, believe the present conflict will widen the gulf between the Arabs and the West. "As the U.S. destroys Iraq it will give birth to the *jihad* (holy war) that will destroy the West," Abbadi warns.[15] Yet others believe a U.S. victory will result in closer Arab ties to the West. Author Dave Hunt predicts that Hussein's war will weaken Arab solidarity and pave the way for unprecedented cooperation with the "new world order."[16]

The crisis in the Middle East has certainly raised new questions about biblical prophecy regarding the continued return of the Jews to Israel, rebuilding the temple, and the whole issue of Arab-Israeli relations. Prophetic speculation is running rampant to say the least! Almost everyone wants to point to some possible prophetic fulfillment in the current crisis.

ARE WE RUNNING OUT OF TIME?

Certainly, war in the Middle East ought to get our attention. For anyone who takes the Bible seriously, there can be little doubt that we have taken another step closer to the return of Christ. "If God wanted to set the stage for the end, He couldn't have done it any better," one prophecy scholar told me recently as we were discussing the situation.

Yet there are still many unanswered questions facing us: Where do we go from here? What attitude should Christians take toward the Middle East? What about Arabs and the Kurds of northern Iraq helplessly caught in the middle? Is Iraq the Babylon of prophecy? What about the Antichrist? How near is the end?

John Walvoord, former president of Dallas Theological Seminary, notes: "The rapidly increasing tempo of change in modern life has given the entire world a sense of impending crisis."[17] He too raises the difficult questions about how long the world can survive until a madman has nuclear bombs or how long the world economic struggle can be held in check before it ends in a bloodbath.

We are facing the most critical days in the history of mankind. The proliferation of nuclear weapons, the depletion of the earth's resources, and man's general mismanagement of the environment all tell us that we are running out of time. Jesus Christ Himself predicted that one day the "times of the Gentiles" will be "fulfilled" (Luke 21:24).

As the prophetic clock continues to tick away, many feel that we have passed the point of no return. They believe the march to Armageddon has already begun. A recent article in *U.S. News & World Report,* entitled, "A Revelation in the Middle East," examined the possibility that the crisis in the Persian Gulf may be a fulfillment of biblical prophecy. Such prominent evangelicals as Billy Graham, Pat Robertson, and Jack Van Impe were cited along with Brooklyn rabbi Manachem Schneerson, leader of the radical orthodox Lubavitchers.[18]

Apocalyptic speculation has been a favorite theological enterprise throughout most of church history. It really took off during the Middle Ages as Catholic theologians envisioned a great end-times battle with the Mohammedan hordes. Even such Protestant stalwarts as Luther and Melanchthon speculated on the date of the end of the world, suggesting that the Turks would be overthrown in the final conflict. In British circles, everyone from Sir Walter Raleigh to John Owen, the Puritan divine, took a stab at prophetic speculation. During the peak of the English Civil War, current events were paralleled with biblical prophecies and dates were set almost weekly—1666 being a favorite of many.[19]

In more recent times, prophetic speculation sold a lot of copies of Harry Rimmer's *The Shadow of Coming Events* (1943), which included his highly influential chapter, "The Coming War with Russia."[20] Rimmer predicted the Allied victory, the defeat of Germany, Italy's loss of her African colonies, including Libya and Ethiopia, and the rise of Russia as a world power. He also foresaw the reestablishment of Israel and the eventual Arab vs. Israel conflict. Rimmer's ideas dominated eschatological thinking at places like Dallas Seminary, where they were studied and reshaped by Hal Lindsey in his best-selling *Late Great Planet Earth* in the 1970s.

Now speculation is running at high tide again. The current crisis may well lead toward end-time events, but we dare not assume more than the Bible actually predicts. The *facts* of prophecy are clear, but the *assumptions* we draw from those facts and the *speculations* we make off those assumptions are another matter. Just because the end is near doesn't necessarily mean the end is here.

2

THE MARCH TO ARMAGEDDON

As the bombs began bursting over Baghdad at 12:50 A.M. on January 17, 1991, President George Bush summoned Marlin Fitzwater, press secretary, to the White House. Fitzwater read the President's official statement to the assembled press at 7:06 P.M., still January 16 in Washington, D.C. He announced, "The liberation of Kuwait has begun."

The era of modern-televised warfare had also begun. For the next several days, Americans and much of the rest of the world sat transfixed by live telecasts that were instantly relayed by satellite from such distant places as Baghdad, Iraq; Riyadh, Saudi Arabia; Amman, Jordan; and Tel Aviv and Jerusalem, Israel.

The era of global communications has been with us for some time, but suddenly we were experiencing it firsthand. With global technology comes the psychological realization that nothing is really faraway anymore. Jet airplanes, television cameras, satellite technology, and long-distance telephones bring the world to our doorstep every day.

For the first time in history, we could watch people use live television as a two-way communications system. Instead of a day-old videotape carried by jet from Vietnam, we were watching Tom Brokaw, Dan Rather, and Peter Jennings talking live with correspondents all over the world.

The instantaneous nature of mass communication brought the distant conflict right into our living rooms. The public seemed captivated, however, not only by the war itself, but by the ominous prospect which it seemed to foreshadow—the possibility of nuclear holocaust in the Middle East. Indeed, it seems to many that Armageddon is on our doorstep.

THE GUNS OF AUGUST

When Saddam Hussein ordered the invasion of Kuwait on August 2, 1990, he unleashed the guns of August that would result in the bombs of winter, beginning in January 1991. Just when the world wanted to congratulate itself for ending the Cold War and ushering in a new world order of peace and prosperity, Hussein upset the global balance of power.

Wars in the Middle East are nothing new. They have been going on for centuries, but this one got the attention of students of Bible prophecy because of Iraq's unprovoked attack on Israel. Many people believe that a war to end all wars will be fought in the Middle East at the end of the age—just before Jesus Christ returns to earth.

The recent crisis precipitated by Iraq's invasion of Kuwait and the rapid deployment of troops by the United Nations coalition reminded all of us how tentative peace really is in that part of the world. Hussein's cry for a Muslim "holy war" against Israel and the foreign devils from the West shows how quickly the dawn of peace can turn to the thunderheads of war.

Many Christians believe that the only resolution to the ongoing conflict will be a peace treaty backed up and enforced by a powerful military leader who will bring the world back from the brink of disaster.[1] A Middle East peace settlement is clearly predicted in Daniel 9:25-27, and other prophecies from this passage have already been fulfilled. Daniel predicted the rebuilding of Jerusalem "in times of trouble," which was done in the days of Nehemiah. He then looked down the corridor of time and saw the Anointed One (Messiah) "cut off." Looking even farther, beyond the death of Christ, Daniel predicted, "War will continue until the end" (Daniel 9:26). And so it has!

THE PROSPECT OF PEACE

The intensity of the Arab-Israeli conflict goes deeper than just the Palestinian question. Certainly this is an important issue in the current debate, but the wanton attack on Israel by Iraq shows the depth of a deeply embedded hatred that will not easily be resolved. This points to the need for a peaceful settlement of gigantic proportions.

The Prophet Daniel predicted the rise of a future world leader who will sign a peace treaty ("covenant," Daniel 9:27) with Israel, presumably for seven years, but will break that agreement at the halfway mark and attack Israel. While Bible scholars have debated the interpretation of this passage for centuries, it seems to speak of an era not unlike our own. Daniel tells us of a future age when knowledge and travel will increase (Daniel 12:4). He seems to have a global picture in mind.

Daniel also predicted an alliance of ten nations growing out of the old Roman Empire (Daniel 7:7-24), symbolized by the ten horns of the creature that represents the last world system. Walvoord suggests, "The final confederacy of ten nations will constitute the revived Roman Empire, which will have the economic and political power necessary to control the Mediterranean."[2]

The unification of the European Economic Community (or Common Market) in 1992 may be a serious step in the direction of a global economy. This EEC dream has been a long time coming since it was first proposed after World War II and formalized by the Rome Treaty in 1957, calling for the eventual economic and political union of the United States of Europe.[3] Since Bible prophecy points to a final economic, military, and political giant that sits on seven hills (e.g., Rome), one has to wonder if we are not now witnessing the formulation of the final alignment of nations at the end of the age.

IS THE COLD WAR REALLY OVER?

For almost three decades the Berlin Wall (1961–1989) festered as a hideous twenty-six-mile-long cement scar across the heart of Europe. Then, in an almost unbelievable moment, the great barrier between East and West Germany came tumbling down. Germans who had been politically segregated for more than a generation found themselves streaming through the Brandenburg Gate into each other's arms. It was one of history's great moments.

The fall of the wall made us all realize how much our lives had been affected by World War II, for its consequences reached across the decades to our own time. But then, at the stroke of midnight, November 9, 1989, it was over. In an act of spontaneous and creative destruction, Berliners from both sides of the wall began breaking it into pieces and pulling it down. The wall itself seem to disappear beneath the waves of humanity which swept over it. *Time* magazine heralded the news: "They tooted trumpets and danced on top. They brought out hammers and chisels and whacked away at the symbol of their imprisonment, knocking loose chunks of concrete and waving them triumphantly before the television cameras."[4]

The Berlin Wall was not the only thing to fall that night. The old order of Europe collapsed as well. The abdication of old communist regimes in Eastern Europe and the prospects for change in the Soviet Union seemed to spell the disappearance of the Iron Curtain once and for all. The "wall of shame," as John F. Kennedy once called it, was gone. So too was the distinction between East and West Germany. For the first time since the days of Adolph Hitler, German reunification became a reality.

Newsweek said: "For Europe, the 1980s ended in a blaze of hope and glory."[5] Communism collapsed and the Soviet satellite nations clamored for democracy. Even within the Soviet Union, the cry for independence was heard from many of the Soviet republics. Yet this sudden and drastic change in the course of history left many people uneasy and asking what it all meant.

To most of the world, Mikhail Gorbachev, leader of the Soviet Union, seemed to be the hero behind the melodrama of change. People quickly forgot that it was Ronald Reagan's resolve to build a stronger America, rearm the military, and stand up to aggression that ultimately spent the Soviets under the table and sent them scurrying for an economic truce.

Subsequent tensions in the Soviet Union have shown that the final solution is yet to be reached. Even Gorbachev's trusted friend, Foreign Secretary Eduard Shevardnadze resigned in protest against the "advance of dictatorship." As Gorbachev moved to consolidate his personal power over the Soviet Union, Shevardnadze warned: "Dictatorship is coming and no one knows what kind of dictatorship it will be."[6]

THERE GOES THE NEIGHBORHOOD

In less than twelve months during 1989, the entire communist bloc of Eastern Europe overthrew its leadership and turned to democracy. The Hungarian parliament voted on January 11 to allow independent political parties. By May 2 Hungarian soldiers began cutting the barbed-wire fence, the literal Iron Curtain, along their country's border with Austria. On May 8 Hungary's communist dictator Janos Kadar was ousted from power, and by October 23 Hungary was an independent republic.

At the same time, the Roman Catholic Church and the Solidarity union joined hands to topple communism in Poland, with union leader Lech Walesa eventually being elected President. Then it began happening like a giant political domino—Czechoslovakia, Bulgaria, and even Romania, where long-time communist dictator Nicolae Ceausescu was assassinated, all broke free from Moscow's control. Mikhail Gorbachev let it happen as the Soviets made no attempt to intervene in Eastern Europe.

The Soviet Union (Russia and her fifteen republics) and Albania now stood alone as the last bastions of communism in Europe. Then came the stormy meeting on Malta between Bush and Gorbachev. There, on the same island where the Apostle Paul was shipwrecked nearly twenty centuries ago (Acts 28:1-10), the two most powerful heads of state met to share a vision of a new world. *Time* flashed the title, "Building a New World" on its cover, with a shot of Bush and Gorbachev smiling as they talked (December 11, 1989).

The earlier "summit" at Reykjavik, Iceland in 1986 opened with Gorbachev producing a list of sweeping arms proposals for Ronald Reagan. But at Malta it was Bush who produced a list of specific demands in the book-lined room on the Soviet cruise liner *Maxim Gorky*. As the winter storm pounded the vessel, the two leaders discussed the end of the Cold War. After sitting silent for most of Bush's hour-long presentation, Gorbachev said, "I have heard you say that you want *perestroika* to succeed, but frankly, I didn't know this. Now I know."[7]

A NEW WORLD ORDER?

When Gorbachev and Bush began talking about a "new world order," evangelical Christians sat up and took careful notice.[8] "What do they mean?" they asked one another. Are they only talking about a post-Cold War world with increased global technology and peaceful international cooperation, or are they talking about the political, economic, and even religious union that the Scripture warns against in the last days?

To the secular press this all sounded like good news. Finally, the two world heavyweights were going to take off their boxing gloves and try to shake hands. Certainly, peace is preferred to war or even the possibility of war. Christians and non-Christians alike must rejoice over the thaw in the Cold War and give peace a chance. But biblically perceptive evangelicals also view this peace as tentative and temporary at best. It is the height of naiveté to think that depraved, sinful human beings can solve their own conflicts apart from God.

Any previous attempts at structuring a world order have always fallen on the harsh realities of man's pride, arrogance, greed, avarice, and self-destruction. Woodrow Wilson's League of Nations failed to stop World War II, and the present United Nations has struggled since its very inception. Yet there seems to be something within the international community propelling us toward a unified world system. Many fear that driving force is Satan himself.

THE ROMAN CONNECTION

En route to Malta, Gorbachev stopped at Rome for the first ever meeting of a Soviet leader with a pope. It was a momentous occasion and may have marked the beginning of some kind of reconciliation between the atheistic Soviet Union and the Roman Catholic and Russian Orthodox churches. It was another of those shocking events that hit so quickly and unexpectedly that we could hardly believe it. The leader of a party and nation formally committed to atheism was calling Pope John Paul II "your holiness" as they conferred for seventy-five minutes in the library of the sixteenth-century Apostolic Palace at the Vatican.

"We need spiritual values," Gorbachev had declared the day before in his remarks in Rome's city hall, where the Treaty of Rome, establishing the European Community, had been signed in 1957.[9] It seemed so well programmed that one might wonder if Satan himself were calling the shots.

The Soviet leader meeting with the pope promised greater religious freedom and included talk about spiritual values! It all sounded too familiar to evangelical Christians who fear a political, economic, and social alliance of Europe with the heads of formal religion. "Doesn't the Bible warn us against both a political and religious Antichrist in the last days?" a friend asked me at the time, expressing great concern.

The Book of Revelation especially predicts the coming

beast with ten horns and seven heads (Revelation 13:1) which embodies the characteristics of Daniel's prophecy (Daniel 7) of the empires of the lion, bear, and leopard. In other words, this coming world power will be the personification and embodiment of the whole history of world powers.[10] It will also be empowered by Satan ("the dragon") himself (Revelation 13:2). Whoever or whatever this "Beast coming out of the sea" (Revelation 13:1) is, he openly blasphemes God and makes war on the saints of God. Yet "all inhabitants of the earth will worship the Beast" (Revelation 13:8).

The Revelation (called in Greek the "Apocalypse") also points to "another beast, coming out of the earth" who looks like a lamb but talks like a dragon (Revelation 13:11). The uniqueness of the second beast is that he is able to get all the inhabitants of the earth to "worship the first Beast" (Revelation 13:12). He deceives the inhabitants of earth and causes them to worship the "image of the first Beast" (Revelation 13:15) and to receive his mark, so that "no one could buy or sell unless he had the mark, which is the name of the Beast or the number of his name" (Revelation 13:17).

Certainly, this prophecy speaks of the religious, political, and economic control of the world at the end of the age by a combination of political and religious powers. The Revelation also depicts this power as "the great prostitute" (Revelation 17:1ff). She too is associated with the Beast's seven heads and ten horns (Revelation 17:3). Since the time of the Reformation in the sixteenth century, Protestants have tended to view her as the Roman Catholic Church. The prophecy itself says, "The seven heads are seven hills on which the woman sits" (Revelation 17:9). The ten horns are "ten kings who have not yet received a kingdom" (Revelation 17:12) but will do so in connection with the Beast. Thus, they are clearly predicted as something yet to come in the future.

MAKING SENSE OF PROPHECY

One of the most difficult tasks in biblical interpretation has been that of discerning the prophecies of the end times. First, we must remember that the people of Jesus' day missed many of the predictions of His first coming. Therefore, we must not presume that we have figured out all the prophetic details of His second coming. Second, we must guard against the great temptation to read prophecy through the eyes of the present. This has been a great difficulty throughout church history. As early as the second century A.D., Montanus predicted Christ would return to set up His kingdom in Phrygia in Asia Minor. Since then, other candidates for the "New Jerusalem" have included Rome, Constantinople, Münster, London, Boston, Chicago, and Salt Lake City.

I have been a Christian now for forty years, and I have heard it all. Every imaginable speculation has arisen as to the identity of the Antichrist, the date of the Rapture, and the beginning of the Battle of Armageddon. Trying to make sense of all this, let me suggest a simple paradigm:

Facts. There are the clearly stated facts of prophetic revelation: Christ will return for His own; He will judge the world; there will be a time of great trouble on the earth at the end of the age; the final conflict will be won by Christ; etc. These basic facts are clearly stated in Scripture.

Assumptions. Factual prophecy only tells us so much and no more. Beyond that we must make certain assumptions. If these are correct, they will lead to valid conclusions, but if not, they may lead to ridiculous speculations. For example, it is an assumption that Russia will invade Israel in the last days. Whether or not that is factual depends on the legitimacy of one's interpretation of Ezekiel's Magog prophecy (Ezekiel 38–39). It is foolish to say we don't need to worry about Russia because it will be destroyed. That is only an assumption.

Speculations. These are purely calculated guesses based on one's assumptions. In many cases they have no basis in prophetic fact at all. For example, the Bible predicts the number of the Antichrist as "666" (Revelation 13:18). We must try to assume what this means. It is an assumption that it is a literal number that will appear on things in the last days. When one prominent evangelist saw the number 666 prefixed on automobile license plates in Israel a few years ago, he speculated that the "mark of the beast" had already arrived in the Holy Land.

The greatest danger of all in trying to interpret biblical prophecy is to assume that our speculations are true and preach them as facts.[11] This has often caused great embarrassment and confusion. For example, when Benito Mussolini rose to power in Rome in the 1920s, many evangelicals assumed he might be the Antichrist who would rule the world from the city of seven hills in the last days. Some even speculated that Adolph Hitler, who rose to power later in Germany, was the false prophet. Others were sure the false prophet was the pope, who was also in Rome.

The time has come when serious students of biblical prophecy must be very clear about what is fact, what is assumption, and what is speculation in matters of prophecy. For example, just because a war breaks out in the Middle East does not mean that war will necessarily lead to Armageddon. Just because modern geopolitical Iraq includes the ruins of ancient Babylon does not necessarily mean that Iraq will be the "Babylon" of the last days.

I heard someone say the other day that Baghdad will be destroyed and Babylon will be rebuilt as the capital of Iraq and finally it will become the new home of the United Nations.

That is pure speculation! It assumes that prophetic "Babylon" is Iraq, then speculates that it will be rebuilt and that the United Nations must move there in order to set up one world government.

Anything is possible, but that does not mean something is probable. The "Babylon" of prophecy (Revelation 17–18) sounds, in some ways, more like the United States or Europe than Iraq. Both the U.S. and Europe are rich and prosperous, yet immoral and corrupt at the same time. Babylon is described as a place where merchants go by ship (Revelation 18:17) to buy their goods and materials: gold, silver, jewelry, clothing, perfumes, and food. Yet in one hour, this great place is destroyed.

The issue at stake is not whether Babylon is the United States, Europe, or Iraq, or whether Magog is Russia or Iran, or even whether the Antichrist is a person or a system (or both). The issue at stake is that we are careful to distinguish between the *facts* of prophecy and our own *assumptions* and *speculations*.

The greatest *fact* of all is that we who are in Christ have the hope of eternal life. Therefore the Apostle Peter said, "In His great mercy He has given us new birth into a living hope . . . into an inheritance that can never perish, spoil or fade— kept in heaven for you . . . ready to be revealed in the last time" (1 Peter 1:3-5).

IT ALL DEPENDS ON
YOUR INTERPRETATION

One of the unique and complex features of biblical prophecy is that it may be interpreted by different hermeneutical models. Eschatology is the theological term for the study of the "end times." It comes from the Greek word *eschatos*, meaning "last" or "last things." Thus, it is used as a broad designation for biblical prophecy.

Within the Christian church there have been a variety of approaches to the study of eschatology. More liberal Protestants refuse to consider it at all, preferring to dismiss prophecy as hopelessly confusing or generally irrelevant. But among evangelicals, prophecy has always been taken seriously. Jesus Christ Himself predicted His return to earth as well as several significant end-time events (Matthew 24–25).

The issue at stake among evangelicals has generally involved *how* one interprets prophecy.[12] Three main schools of thought have been proposed. While most evangelicals are premillennialists in their view of eschatology, amillennial and postmillennial options also exist.

Postmillennial. This school of thought believes that the Millennium (1,000 years of Revelation 20:1-3) is to be inter-

Postmillennial Scheme

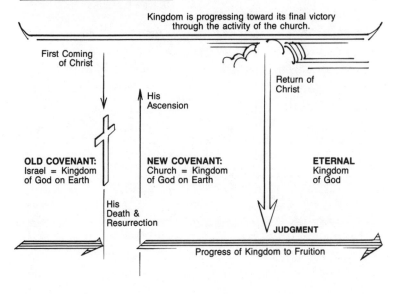

Kingdom is progressing toward its final victory through the activity of the church.

First Coming of Christ

His Ascension

Return of Christ

OLD COVENANT:
Israel = Kingdom of God on Earth

NEW COVENANT:
Church = Kingdom of God on Earth

ETERNAL Kingdom of God

His Death & Resurrection

JUDGMENT

Progress of Kingdom to Fruition

preted symbolically as synonymous with the Church Age. Satan's power is viewed as being "bound" by the power of the Gospel. Postmillennialists believe that during this "Millennium" (Church Age) the church is called upon to conquer unbelief, convert the masses, and govern society by the mandate of biblical law. Only after Christianity succeeds on earth will Christ return and announce that His kingdom has been realized. Postmillennial advocates have included Catholics, Puritans, charismatics, and dominionists who urge believers to take dominion over the earth and its political governments in order to actualize the kingdom of God on earth.[13]

Amillennial. This approach sees no Millennium of any kind on the earth. Rather, amillennialists tend to view so-called millennial prophecies as being fulfilled in eternity. References to the "thousand years" are interpreted symbolically. In this scheme the Church Age ends with the return of

Amillennial Scheme

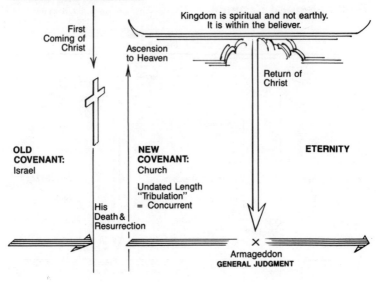

First Coming of Christ

Kingdom is spiritual and not earthly. It is within the believer.

Ascension to Heaven

Return of Christ

OLD COVENANT: Israel

NEW COVENANT: Church

Undated Length "Tribulation" = Concurrent

His Death & Resurrection

ETERNITY

Armageddon
GENERAL JUDGMENT

Christ to judge the world and usher in eternity. God's promises to Israel are viewed as having been fulfilled in the church (the New Israel of the New Covenant); therefore, amillennialists see no specific future for national Israel. They view the Church Age as the era of conflict between the forces of good and evil which culminates with the return of Christ.[14]

Premillennial. This view holds that Christ will return at the end of the Church Age in order to set up His kingdom on earth for a literal 1,000 years.[15] Most also believe there will be a Great Tribulation period on earth prior to the return of Christ. Among premillennialists are those who believe the church will go through the Tribulation (post-Tribulationists) and those who believe the church will be raptured prior to the Tribulation (pre-Tribulationists) and even a few who believe the church will be raptured in the middle of the Tribulation (mid-Tribulationists).[16] Despite these differences

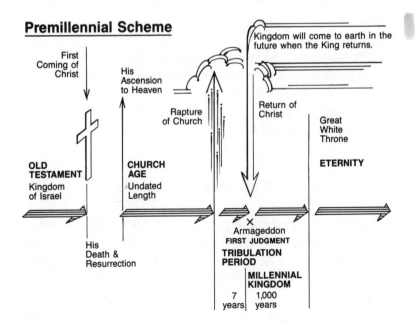

Premillennial Scheme

Kingdom will come to earth in the future when the King returns.

First Coming of Christ

His Ascension to Heaven

Rapture of Church

Return of Christ

Great White Throne

OLD TESTAMENT
Kingdom of Israel

CHURCH AGE
Undated Length

ETERNITY

His Death & Resurrection

×
Armageddon
FIRST JUDGMENT
TRIBULATION PERIOD
MILLENNIAL KINGDOM
7 years | 1,000 years

in regard to the Rapture of the church, premillennialists generally believe in the future restoration of the state of Israel and the eventual conversion of the Jews to Christianity.

Most evangelicals hold to the dispensational premillennial view of eschatology which looks forward to the Rapture ("translation" or "absorption" of believers to heaven) as the next major prophetic event. This, they believe, will end the Church Age and prepare the way for the Tribulation Period and the return of Christ. The Rapture is suggested by such biblical passages as Paul's words to the Thessalonians: "For the Lord Himself will come down from heaven, with a loud command, with the voice of the archangel and with the trumpet call of God, and the dead in Christ will rise first. After that, we who are still alive and are left will be caught up with them in the clouds to meet the Lord in the air. And so we will be with the Lord forever" (1 Thessalonians 4:16-17).

Commenting on the Rapture of the church, David Jeremiah writes:

> When Jesus Christ returns for His own, the world will not hear the voice nor the trumpet. The ears of nonbelievers will be deaf and their eyes blind. It will take place so fast, "in the twinkling of an eye," that no one left behind will understand what has happened.[17]

THE END IS COMING

Whatever one's eschatological preference may be, evangelical Christians take seriously Bible prophecies about the end times, the Great Tribulation, Armageddon, and the return of Christ. We are genuinely convinced that the march to Armageddon, the last great battle, has already begun. Many believe we are living in the "end times" when the world will be plunged into a series of cataclysmic wars that may well claim three-fourths of the world's population.

However, just because evangelicals believe such prophecies does not mean they want to hasten these events. In the 1984 Presidential debates, Marvin Kalb asked Ronald Reagan, "Do you think we are now heading, perhaps, for some kind of nuclear Armageddon?"[18] Recently even a considerable portion of the secular community has agreed that we seem to be approaching the end of the world. Nobel laureates and reputable scientists have warned that the earth's time clock is running out. Air and water pollution, the evaporation of the protective ozone layer, the elimination of oxygen-producing rain forests, and the general instability of the earth's crust have all been cited as serious problems for the future of life on this planet.

In past centuries, when evangelicals talked about the end of the world, people laughed at them because the destruction of the entire planet was simply inconceivable. But today it is well within the realm of possibility for the Christian and agnostic alike. The gloomy apocalyptic vision of Jonathan Schell's *Fate of the Earth* is an example of such concern.[19]

The Bible warns us that the "Day of the Lord will come like a thief in the night" (1 Thessalonians 5:1-2). It will be a sudden and instantaneous act which will catch the world unprepared. In fact, the Bible reminds us that just people will promise, "'Peace, peace' ... when there is no peace" (Jeremiah 8:11; Ezekiel 13:10).

Mankind has demonstrated irrevocably that it cannot bring a permanent and lasting peace to this world. Every human effort at peace has been short-lived and destined to failure. At the end of time, when the stakes are the highest, the greatest gamble for peace ever made will end in the greatest battle of all time—at Armageddon.

THE COMING DARKNESS

Nearly 2,000 years have passed since Jesus promised, "I will come back" (John 14:3). Throughout subsequent generations of church history, believers have held tenaciously to this promise. It has become to the church what the Apostle Paul called, "that blessed hope, and the glorious appearing of the great God and our Savior Jesus Christ" (Titus 2:13, KJV).

Behind the facts of history, Christians see a great spiritual conflict with the powers of darkness.[20] God has clearly been at work in human history, but so has Satan. Humankind has produced its saints and its sinners, its Florence Nightingales and its Adolph Hitlers. Secular history views mankind's supposed evolving struggle with God left out of the picture. By contrast, sacred history views God as a part of the natural or historical process. Christianity begins with the presupposition that God is at work in history. In fact, Christian theology insists that God has already intervened in human history in the incarnation of Christ.

The Soviet exile and Christian believer Aleksandr Solzhenitsyn clearly understood this when he wrote:

> All of us are standing on the brink of a great historical cataclysm, a flood that swallows up civilization and changes whole epochs. The present world situation is complicated still more by the fact that several hours have struck simultaneously on the clock of history.[21]

The great transitions of the last 2,000 years have changed the course of history:

> Conversion of Constantine
> Fall of Rome
> Rise of the Papacy
> Mohammed and the Rise of Islam

Middle Ages
Renaissance
Reformation
Industrial Revolution
Modern Technological Explosion

Each of these transitions thrust humanity into a new era of human experience. In each transition, the old world seemed to fade away as it was replaced by a new world order. Many believe that we are now on the brink of such a transition again—this time to a global world. One economy, a global economy, will soon replace our national economies. One government, an international cooperative body, will overshadow individual governments—even our own. Finally, one religion, an apostate form of pseudo-Christianity, will unite the religious world. There may be exceptions here and there—a few evangelicals, the Muslims, and certainly the Jews. But the prophecies of the end times indicate they will come under persecution by the leader of the world system.

CAN ANYONE SAVE US?

Modern man has reached the point in his intellectual journey where he does not want to face the logical consequences of a secular world without God. But instead of turning to God, people are now turning to a kind of scientific mysticism that has been popularized as the New Age movement. This trendy new approach to religion without rules combines transcendentalism, spiritualism, Oriental mysticism, and transpersonal psychology. At the heart of the New Age movement is the worship of the Planet Earth (the mother goddess, Gaia). A popular children's television cartoon, "Captain Planet," projects this propaganda in animated form every Saturday morning.

Modern man has come to the realization that he needs hope. Despite his rejection of Christ as the Savior of the world, modern man must hold onto something beyond himself. He often personalizes that hope as some kind of super hero (Superman, Batman, Rocky, or Rambo). Everyone wants to believe that someone will come along and save the world from destruction. However, the Bible makes it clear that only one person will ever come to save the world, and that is Jesus Christ!

In the meantime, the gathering storm on the human horizon looks more ominous all the time. The instability of the world economy has business leaders worried all over the world. The realignment of nations on the European continent leaves many questions still unanswered about the future of Europe. The continued strife in the Middle East unnerves us all when we realize how quickly the march to Armageddon could begin.

3

THE END IS NEAR
... OR IS IT?

Questions about the second coming of Christ and the end of
the world are not new. Jesus' own disciples raised three such
questions themselves. Toward the end of His earthly ministry, Jesus predicted the destruction of Jerusalem and the temple they all held so dear. Matthew 24–25 contains Jesus' last
major discourse and His clearest statements about the future.
His message included a prediction of the imminent fall of
Jerusalem and also pointed to the distant future when the
"times of the Gentiles" would come to an end during the
Great Tribulation.

The disciples were awed by the spectacular architecture of
the temple in Jerusalem and commented on it to Jesus. To
their amazement, He replied that "not one stone here will be
left on another; every one will be thrown down" (Matthew
24:2). Stunned by this remark, the disciples asked their Lord
three questions:

1. "When will this happen?"
2. "What will be the sign of Your coming?"
3. "And of the end of the age?" (Matthew 24:3)

As He sat on the Mount of Olives, opposite the temple precincts, Jesus answered those questions in what has been called the Olivet Discourse. Thus, His entire message is looked on as the answer to these three questions. John Walvoord comments, "Premillenarians, accordingly, interpret the discourse as an accurate statement of end-time events, which will lead up to and climax in the second coming of Christ to set up His millennial kingdom on earth."[1]

The key to interpreting this passage rests in one's view of the "Gospel of the kingdom" (Matthew 24:13-14). Since Matthew has already shown in his parables that the present form of the kingdom is the church, it seems proper to interpret the events in this discourse as relating to the entire Church Age and culminating dramatically toward the end of that age. Therefore, John could say, in Revelation 1:9, that he was a "companion in tribulation, and in the kingdom," though he was still in the Church Age. Thus, the "signs" (Greek, *semeion*) of the end are general characteristics of the present age which shall be intensified as this age moves toward its conclusion. These are followed by more specific signs (Matthew 24:15-26) of the Tribulation Period and the final return of Christ in judgment (Matthew 24:27-31).

SIGNS OF THE TIMES

Jesus warned His followers not to be deceived by the host of false prophets and false messiahs who would follow in a long parade throughout the Church Age. He also warned of "wars and rumors of wars" (Matthew 24:6) that would follow throughout the present era and have continually marked the "age of the Gentiles." Such wars do *not* in themselves indicate that the end is near. These are only the "beginning of birth pangs" (Matthew 24:8). Such conflicts may point to the end, but serious Bible students dare not interpret any one conflict as necessarily "prophetic" of the end times. In reality, every war that occurs on earth during this present era is a fulfillment of this prophecy.

Despite such wars, Jesus warned in Matthew 24:6, "The end is still to come" ("the end is not yet" [kjv]). Unfortunately, many people miss this point altogether. They read about wars, earthquakes, and natural disasters and conclude that the end must be near. Yet Jesus Himself said such is not the case.

Thus the war with Iraq cannot be viewed as necessarily a fulfillment of prophecy, though it may be a step in that direction. This is precisely where Bible students need to be careful not to jump from the *facts* of prophecy to their well-intended *assumptions* and finally to pure *speculations.*

Everything listed in this part of Jesus' response—wars, famines, and earthquakes—is to be expected throughout the Church Age until He returns. These are the "beginning of birth pains" (Matthew 24:8), but they do not in themselves prove the final fulfillment is about to be delivered.

Every crisis in the Middle East—1948, 1956, 1967, 1973, and 1991—has led to similar prophetic speculations with sincere teachers announcing that the end is just around the corner. What the recent crisis shows is that the old animosities have not died out and the potential for a major Arab alliance against Israel in the Last Days is still a very real possibility in the future—but that future could be a month, a year, ten years, or a hundred years from now.

THE END OF THE AGE

Jesus stated that the end of the age would come when the "Gospel of the kingdom" has been preached "in the whole world as a testimony to all nations" (Matthew 24:14). The proclamation of the Gospel is not precisely defined as to whether it is *announced* to all the world (Greek, *oikoumenē*, "inhabited world") and every nation (Greek, *ethnos*, "Gentile nations") or whether it is *believed* in every nation. But one fact is clear: Christ's Great Commission to evangelize the world (Matthew 28:18-20) is to be carried out faithfully until He returns. Christ's later warning (Matthew 24:36) that no one knows the time of His return emphasizes that we are to continue faithfully doing what He commanded until He comes.

The end (Greek, *telos*) that shall come after the proclamation of the Gospel is the end of the Church Age, which parallels the "times of the Gentiles" during the present era. While some commentators limit the events in this passage to the Tribulation Period, it seems clear that they are occurring throughout the entire Church Age as the Gospel is preached primarily to the Gentiles.[2]

Eschatology is the study of the end times and is generally associated with the study of biblical prophecies of future events. Jesus spoke of the "end of the age" in response to His disciples' questions. There can be no doubt that He viewed human history as moving toward a final climax, not as an endless cycle of repetitive events. William S. LaSor notes that the Jews of the Intertestamental Period distinguished between "this age" (Hebrew, *haùolam hazzeh*) and "the age to come" (Hebrew, *haùolam habbah*). Thus, LaSor concludes that the expression "the end of the world" comes from Judeo-Christian roots and is understood by both Jews and Christians as referring to this world (or age) coming to an end and being replaced by the age to come.[3]

A similar concept is found in the Old Testament expression "the latter days" (Hebrew, *be'aharit hayyamim*). Moses foretold the future apostasy of Israel, her scattering, and her return to the Lord in the "latter days" (Deuteronomy 4:30; cf. 31:29, KJV). The Prophet Hosea spoke of the future repentance of Israel in the "latter days" (Hosea 3:5, KJV). The Prophet Jeremiah predicted numerous events that would occur in the "latter days" (Jeremiah 23:20; 30:24; 48:47; 49:39, KJV). Ezekiel predicted the invasion of Israel by a coalition of nations ("Gog and Magog") in the "latter days" (Ezekiel 38:16, KJV), also using the alternate expression "in the latter years" (Ezekiel 38:8, KJV).

It was against this Old Testament backdrop that our Lord spoke to His disciples about the coming end of the world. His warnings about false prophets, counterfeit messiahs, natural disasters, and persecution have proven true time and time again throughout the Church Age.

THE GREAT TRIBULATION

As Jesus looked down the corridor of time to the end of the present age—an age which would be launched by the preaching of the Gospel of His death and resurrection and by the empowerment of His disciples with the Holy Spirit—He warned of a time of great tribulation ("great distress" [Matthew 24:21, NIV]) which would come upon the whole world (Matthew 24:15-28). The "abomination of desolation" (Matthew 24:15, KJV) refers to when Antiochus Epiphanes profaned Jewish temple worship during the Intertestamental Period (Daniel 9:27; 11:31; 12:11), foreshadowing an even more serious abomination that would yet occur in the future. Whereas Antiochus offered an unclean pig on the sacred altar of the temple, the Antichrist will offer himself! (2 Thessalonians 2:4)

The act of desecration which Daniel had predicted about Antiochus, the pagan Hellenistic ruler, will be repeated even more seriously in the future as the signal of the beginning of the Great Tribulation on earth. Since Jesus saw this as still in the future, such an abomination is not limited to the past actions of Antiochus. Nor was it fulfilled merely in the Roman destruction of Jerusalem in A.D. 70, since our Lord called it "Great Tribulation" (KJV) that is "unequaled from the beginning of the world until now—and never to be equaled again" (Matthew 24:21). Our Lord went on to explain that the devastation of the Great Tribulation will be so awful that unless those days were cut short, "no one would survive" (Matthew 24:22).

Jesus further described this coming time of trouble ("distress," NIV) as a time when the sun and moon are darkened and the heavens shall be shaken (Matthew 24:29). His description runs parallel to that found in Revelation 16:1-16 where the final hour of the earth's Tribulation is depicted by atmospheric darkness, air pollution, and ecological disaster. These cataclysmic events accompany the return of Christ at the end of the Tribulation Period.

Christ's return to earth will be marked by "the sign of the Son of man" appearing in the sky (Matthew 24:30). This sign is not explained in this passage. Ancient commentators, like Chrysostom, thought it might be the appearance of a cross in the sky. More recent commentators tend to follow Lange's view that it is the Shekinah glory of the divine Christ.[4]

Remember our paradigm from the previous chapters: facts, assumptions, speculations.

> **Fact.** Christ will return after the Tribulation Period, and the sign of the Son of man will appear in heaven.
>
> **Assumption.** Christ will return after a seven-year Tribulation Period and be seen by all the peoples of the earth.
>
> **Speculation.** (1) The "sign" will be the return of the Bethlehem star; (2) it will be the sign of the cross; (3) the sky

will turn blood red, symbolizing the blood of Christ; and (4) the Shekinah glory of God will gradually unfold into blinding splendor.

Any one of these speculations could be true, or none of them may properly explain what will happen when this "sign" appears. Careful students of prophecy dare not push their speculations as facts. If we keep this simple distinction, we can avoid saying more than the Bible actually says about prophetic events.

ILLUSTRATIONS THAT SHOUT

A dear friend of mine always preached with great intensity; even the supplemental comments in his sermons were screamed. However, after he had preached in a chapel service for one of America's outstanding ministries and screamed the whole time at some of the most committed Christian workers in the whole world, he was helped greatly when the leader of that organization gave him this simple advice: "Let the truth be obvious and let the illustrations do the shouting!"

At this point in the Olivet Discourse, Jesus used several effective illustrations ("parables") that clearly shouted the truth He was presenting.

1. *Illustration of the Fig Tree* (Matthew 24:32-35)

Jesus reminded His disciples that they could discern the coming of the end of the age by the illustration of a blossoming fig tree. Our Lord said, "Now learn this lesson from the fig tree: As soon as its twigs get tender and its leaves come out, you know that summer is near" (Matthew 24:32). When a tree blooms in the spring, we discern that summer is coming. "Even so," Jesus added, "when you see all these things, you know that it [My coming] is near, right at the door" (Matthew 24:33).

The immediate context is illustrative of the point our Lord was making about His coming. While Israel at times is symbolized as an olive tree, the usage here seems to be that of an illustration. Just as God has programmed time indicators into nature (e.g., budding trees), so He has programmed into prophetic history certain time indicators of future events.

The generation that lives to see "all these things" come to pass will "not pass away" before Christ returns at the end of the age (Matthew 24:34). This difficult saying has been variously interpreted as (1) being fulfilled in the apostles' own lifetime with the destruction of Jerusalem in A.D. 70; (2) referring to the perpetual survival of the race ("generation") of the Jews; (3) the terminal generation at the time of Christ's return. The Arndt and Gingrich lexicon prefers to translate "generation" (Greek, *genea*) as "age" or "period of time."[5] In other words, the previously listed signs will continue to multiply throughout the Church Age and reach their ultimate climax at the end of the age—in the generation of those who live to see the entire matter fulfilled.

2. *Illustration of the Flood* (Matthew 24:36-39)
Our Lord next turned to the story of Noah and the great Flood to describe the suddenness of His future return. He said, "As it was in the days of Noah, so it will be at the coming of the Son of man" (Matthew 24:37). He went on to describe the immoral, self-indulgent generation of Noah's day as typical of the generation of the Last Days. They "knew nothing about what would happen" until it was too late (Matthew 24:39).

This illustration, drawn from Genesis 6–9, reminds us that we must always be ready for our Lord to return because "no one knows about that day or hour" (Matthew 24:36). This is one of the most important declarations given in all of biblical prophecy, and yet it is constantly violated. "It says we cannot know the 'day' or the 'hour,' but it doesn't say anything about the year," people will often remark. Others try to argue for a deeper sense of knowledge by playing off the different Greek words for "know" used in the New Testament. The *intent* of the text is clear: no one knows when Christ is coming— so stop trying to guess. Make sure you are prepared *whenever* He comes!

Thus, Jesus admonished, "Keep watch" (Matthew 24:42) and "Be ready" (Matthew 24:44) for we do not know when He will come. He never told us to calculate any dates or speculate beyond what Scripture predicts. He told us to "keep watch" (discernment) and "be ready" (determination). These admonitions are followed by three illustrations that tell us to *keep serving:* the Parables of the Two Servants (Matthew 24:43-51) and the Ten Virgins (Matthew 25:1-13) and the Talents of Money (Matthew 25:14-30).

3. Illustrations of the Servants, Virgins, and Money (Matthew 24:43–25:30)
Jesus clearly stated that the "faithful and wise servant" (Matthew 24:45) was the one found faithfully fulfilling his responsibilities when the master returned. C.S. Lewis put it this way: The best place to be when the inspection comes is at your post. By contrast, the evil servant, says Kent, "mistakes the uncertainty of the time of coming for a certainty that it will not be soon."[6]

The Parable of the Ten Virgins (Matthew 25:1-13) conveys the same warning to be prepared when the master comes. These virgins (Greek, *parthenos*) are attendants at the wedding, not the bride, and may symbolize both the saved and unsaved of Israel rather than the church. Nevertheless, the emphasis is still personal preparation and service. Note also the references to "a long time" in Matthew 24:48; 25:5, 19. All three parables contain this phrase. This implies that Jesus (the Master) would be gone for a long period of time before He returned.

3. In the Parable of the Talents (Matthew 25:14-30), our Lord again underscored the importance of faithful service in His absence. The "talents" represent monetary values entrusted to us for use in God's service and symbolize the gifts and abilities He has given us with which to serve Him. The "far country" (Matthew 25:14, KJV) seems to be heaven and, again, the master is gone a long time before returning to call his servants to accountability. The fearful servant who hid the money failed to understand the real generosity of the master who wanted him to experience the joys of service.

All of these illustrations shout one great truth: Keep serving till Jesus comes again. They could not be more clear in their intent, no matter how one interprets the various elements or details of these parables. They remind all of us that we do not know *when* our Lord will return; therefore, we must remain faithful to Him until He comes.

I think the implications of these admonitions are clear:

1. Keep Watching.
2. Stay Ready.
3. Keep Serving.

If you are in college or graduate school, keep studying— don't drop out! What better thing could Christ find you doing than preparing to serve Him. This is no time to drop out in an act of irresponsible desperation. Hit the books and stay at it.

When I was in college, some students were theorizing that the days were short and the end was near. "Why not drop out now," they said, "and give our lives to serving God?" They missed the point that by studying they were serving God— and home they went. It has also occurred to me since then that if they had stayed in school, they might be better equipped today to have a really effective ministry for God.

If you have a job, keep it—don't quit. God may lead you to take a step of faith in His service, but don't take a step of foolishness. Over the years, I have watched many people give up all responsibility "to serve the Lord," only to watch them take it all back on themselves later. Be faithful in your tasks today, and God will open doors of service tomorrow.

If you have a place of service in your local church, keep at it—don't quit. If you are a teacher, keep teaching. If you are in choir, keep singing. If you are an elder, keep ruling. If you are a deacon, keep serving. And if you are a pastor, keep pastoring. As the hymn writer has so beautifully said it: "May He find us faithful."

JESUS AND THE PROPHETS

Jesus' predictions about the end times blend His answers to all three questions raised by His disciples. Obviously, the temple was destroyed by the Romans in A.D. 70, but the preaching of the Gospel to the whole world is still in progress today. Thus, both a near judgment of Jerusalem by the Romans and an ultimate judgment by the Antichrist seem to be in view in this passage. LaSor notes: "But regardless of the sequence intended (or that we impose on the passage), Jesus does mention a great tribulation in connection with the end time events."[7] He further notes that Jesus' reference to the Prophet Daniel definitely connects Him to Israel's prophetic heritage.

Daniel's prophecies (Daniel 2, 7) mention the sequence of four major Gentile world powers that will come in succession: Babylon, Persia, Greece, and Rome. Out of the latter kingdom one will rise who will make "war against the saints"

(Daniel 7:19-21). He is also pictured as one who brings "desolation" and "abomination" (Daniel 9:27). This same imagery is used by our Lord in the New Testament. In Daniel 11:21-31 we read again of the "contemptible person" who profanes the temple with his armed forces to set up the "abomination that causes desolation." From the context of Daniel's prophecies, we conclude that the "time of trouble" or "Great Tribulation" involves Daniel's people, the Jews. We also conclude that the king who "magnifies himself above every God" (Daniel 11:36) is the Antichrist of the last days.

The Prophet Jeremiah also refers to a "time of trouble for Jacob [Israel]" (Jeremiah 30:1-9) in the future. Jeremiah was writing during the Babylonian Captivity and saw in the distant future an even greater time of trouble.

The Book of Revelation pictures the Great Tribulation as both Satan's last desperate attempt to destroy the work of God in creation and salvation and as God's ultimate judgment on the kingdom of Satan as the outpouring of the "wrath of the Lamb" (Revelation 6:16) who is Christ. The Great Tribulation is the final judgment of God against the sin and wickedness on earth and results in the resounding declaration, "It is done!" (literally, "It is finished," Revelation 16:17) The atonement of Christ was finalized with this same declaration on the cross, when He lifted up His head and with a loud voice said, "It is finished" (Matthew 27:50; John 19:30). Now, at the end of the Great Tribulation of God's judgment, the same cry will go up, "It is finished!"

The final act of God's judgment at the end of the Great Tribulation is generally referred to as the Battle of Armageddon (Revelation 16:16). The other biblical term for this final conflict is the "Day of the Lord," which is mentioned several times in the Old Testament prophets.[8] This "day" is viewed by the prophets as a day of darkness and judgment related to the end time.

The Prophet Zechariah pictured the "Day of the Lord" as a time when all the nations will gather together against the city of Jerusalem, and the Lord shall go forth to defend the city and "on that day His feet shall stand on the Mount of Olives, east of Jerusalem, and the Mount of Olives will be split in two from east to west, forming a great valley, with half of the mountain moving north and half moving south" (Zechariah 14:4).

BACK TO THE FUTURE

As we trace the words of Jesus back to the Old Testament prophets, we see that they all point to the future. In a very significant and symbolic gesture, Jesus took His disciples to the Mount of Olives to deliver His most important prophetic message. Not only could they look down on the city of Jerusalem and the temple across the Kidron Valley, but they were sitting on the very mount from which Jesus would ascend back into heaven (Acts 1:12) and to which He will one day return. He will split it in two when He comes to judge the world and deliver His people.

They could not have gone to a more appropriate place to receive Jesus' message about those things pertaining to His second coming and the end of the age. Think of what that mountain has witnessed over the years:

- The conquest of Jerusalem by King David of Israel (c. 1000 B.C.).
- David's retreat from Jerusalem and from Absalom over the Mount of Olives.
- David's return to Jerusalem and the restoration of his throne.
- The splendor of Jerusalem under King Solomon and the building of the temple (971–931 B.C.).

- The subsequent rise and fall of the kings of Judah at Jerusalem (931–586 B.C.).
- The Babylonian Captivity and the destruction of the temple (586 B.C.).
- The Jews' return under Ezra and the rebuilding of the temple by Zerubbabel (515 B.C.).
- Rebuilding of the walls of Jerusalem by Nehemiah (445 B.C.).
- Rome conquering Jerusalem (63 B.C.).
- Temple repaired and expanded (beginning in 20 B.C.).
- Ministry, death, and resurrection of Jesus Christ (A.D. 30–33).
- Temple completed (A.D. 64).
- Destruction of Jerusalem and the temple. Scattering of the Jews (A.D. 70).
- Rise of Islam and building of the Dome of the Rock in honor of Mohammed (A.D. 687–691).
- General Allenby of Great Britain liberating Jerusalem from the Turks and beginning of British protectorate of Palestine (A.D. 1917).
- Israel reestablished as a nation (A.D. 1948).
- Israel gaining full possession of Jerusalem (A.D. 1967).
- Saddam Hussein of Iraq attacking Israel (A.D. 1991).

Yet the greatest prophetic event of all is yet in the future—the return of Jesus Christ to the Mount of Olives! In His Olivet Discourse our Lord promised to return but set no date, though He implied in His illustrations that He would be gone for a long time (Matthew 25:5, 19). He urged His disciples to always be ready for Him to return. Thus, the concept of an imminent and sudden, or unexpected, coming reminds us to "be ready" whenever He might return.

In the meantime, Jesus instructed His disciples to keep serving Him faithfully until He returned. This dual emphasis leaves us with a proper balance about matters of biblical prophecy, the return of Christ, and the end of the age. On the one hand, we are to be watching and ready for Him to come at any moment. On the other hand, we are to continue serving Him for as long as He waits. One preacher put it this way: "Live your life as though He could come today, but plan your work as if you had a hundred years."

The most serious announcement in Jesus' message was that *no one* can set any dates for His return (Matthew 24:36). Yet this has been one of the most violated declarations in Scripture. Over the centuries, well-meaning believers have wanted to assume they were living in the "Last Days." Something in the human psyche makes us want to believe we are the "terminal generation." Perhaps it is a combination of pride about ourselves and our excitement about the coming of Christ that causes us to read the prophecies of the future through the eyes of the present. But whenever believers have done this, they have jumped from the *facts* of prophecy to their own *assumptions* and eventually to wild-eyed *speculations*.

Whenever preachers start saying things like, "It will be over in six years," they are speculating and not preaching. How many times have we read over the years that Babylon was being rebuilt or that Israel was planning to rebuild the temple or that the free world was about to collapse?[9] One well-known prophecy preacher has frequently alluded to dates for the return of Christ, "predicted" the communist flag would fly from Independence Hall in Philadelphia by July 4, 1976, and has often said we only have a few years left. Does anyone object to such speculation or urge caution to such statements? Hardly at all! He has printed pictures of Mount St. Helens exploding and Israeli license plates with 666 prefixed to them and told us again and again that we are out of time. He means well, but does not this kind of blatant speculation cause many people to reject legitimate discussion of prophecy?

Guessing dates and reading our own times into biblical prophecy is a temptation to which Christians have often succumbed. The end is near, but we dare not claim to know that the end is here. Apocalyptic speculation is a difficult and dangerous enterprise when applied to political and social policies. One had better be sure he is right before proceeding with his vision for the end.

4

MISCALCULATING THE SECOND COMING

In the summer of 1988, my telephone rang one Saturday afternoon. I was drinking a cup of coffee and contemplating mowing the grass when the disruption came. A preacher friend of mine in California was all excited about the Rapture happening soon.

"I've just read the most amazing booklet about Bible prophecy!" Randy shouted all the way from the West Coast. "This guy has calculated the events of the end times and predicts the Rapture will occur on September 12, 1988!"

"You've got to be kidding!" I responded. "Those things never work out the way they claim."

"No, this is for real," Randy insisted. "This guy is an engineer and he has spent years working out a detailed calculation based on the Feast of Trumpets (Rosh Hashanah) symbolizing the Rapture."

"I've heard that before," I quipped. "Some guys were saying that back in 1975 and nothing happened. Who is this writer?" I asked.

Randy paused a moment while he scanned the cover of the

booklet. "Edgar Whisenant," he stated somewhat cautiously. "The booklet is entitled, *88 Reasons Why the Rapture Will Be in 1988.*"[1]

"I've never heard of him!" I said sternly as though I expected my voice to indicate some sense of authority and finality. After a few silent seconds, I asked, "Where did you get this booklet?"

"It came in the mail," Randy explained jubilantly. "Everybody is talking about it out here."

"Well, nobody in St. Louis knows anything about it," I assured him.

"Don't you think it's possible that he's right?" Randy asked, pleading for some reasonable consideration on my part.

"Randy, you used to be one of my students," I moaned. "You ought to know better! Just because something is possible doesn't mean it is probable. It is possible that the moon may disappear, but it isn't probable that it will."

Randy was typical of many evangelical Christians. He sincerely believed the Bible, but he wanted to make it say more than it really says. He wanted to believe that he is living in the last days and the events of his time have great prophetic significance. The problem is that Christians have thought that for centuries and have often attempted to read prophecy through the eyes of their own experiences. The result has been a host of miscalculated guesses based on faulty presuppositions.

Evangelicals take seriously the doctrine of the second coming of Christ. We believe that He will literally return to the earth one day to vindicate the church and judge the world. We may differ among ourselves on *when* and *how* He will return, but most of us are convinced He will return as He promised.

Another characteristic of evangelicals is our concept of the imminence of Christ's return. Most of us believe that He could come at any moment. There are exceptions to this, of course, but most evangelicals are expecting Him to come soon. While this hope gives the church great comfort and expectation, it often leads to excessive speculation. Think of all the "candidates" for Antichrist that have been proposed in the twentieth century alone: Kaiser Wilhelm, Mussolini, Hitler, Stalin, Khrushchev, Gorbachev, Henry Kissinger, and Ronald Wilson Reagan (6 letters in each name = 666), plus a host of others.

Suddenly it hit me like a bolt out of the blue! "Randy," I shouted back into the telephone, "how long have you been a Christian?"

"Ten years," he answered, sounding somewhat bewildered.

"That's the problem!" I announced. "You haven't been in evangelical circles long enough to have heard all these other sure-fire predictions that have misfired. You don't have the perspective to evaluate this kind of conjecture."

At that moment, I realized why Christians are so gullible about such things. They just don't know any better. Many of them have only a limited knowledge of biblical prophecy. In most cases they believe whatever position is taken in the church where they were converted. "After all," they theorize, "if our church is right about salvation, we must be right about prophecy too."

I also realized that if pastors, with theological training, could fall for the latest eschatological scam, anyone could! The prospects are frightening. "We are raising a generation of biblical illiterates and theological neophytes who are actually dangerous," I told my wife after I hung up the phone. "These people are so sincere that their pietism has obliterated their sense of reason."

"Why don't you write a book about this," Donna suggested. "Maybe it could help straighten out some of this confusion."

"A book! We don't need another book!" I exclaimed. "Surely someone else will write about this, and I won't have to do it."

Well, time has passed now and things have only gotten worse! No serious word of caution has come forth, and in the meantime, events like the Persian Gulf crisis, the collapse of communism in Eastern Europe, the reunification of Germany, and the prospects of a global economy have brought forth a whole host of prophetic speculators.

EVERYTHING OLD IS NEW AGAIN

Eschatological excitement and prophetic panic tend to go hand in hand. Every time a war heats up in the Middle East, there will be a number of "prophetic panhandlers" assuring us that this is the big one. Despite the church's twenty-century-long struggle to understand biblical prophecy, these modern-day "prophets" claim to have it all figured out—some to the very day!

Most evangelicals hold the reformers and Puritans in high esteem as great theologians and Bible expositors of the grace of God and rightly so.[2] Therefore, it comes as a great surprise that their eschatological speculations were about as bizarre as any that may be offered today. However, given their historical frame of reference and certain *assumptions* of their times, it is easy to see how they developed *speculations* about the coming of Christ and the end of the world, which they viewed as about to come at any moment.

Date-setting and speculation about the end times is an old habit. Many of the reformers believed they were living in the Last Days, that Satan had been loosed, and that the Antichrist sought to extend his rule over the whole world by means of the Roman Catholic papacy. The idea had been developed during the Middle Ages that Satan was bound for a thousand years, approximately A.D. 300–1300. During this time, from the reign of Constantine until the time of the Reformation, the Gospel spread throughout Europe virtually unhindered.[3]

Anselm of Havelburg (died 1158) was probably the first to suggest that the seven seals of Revelation represent the seven ages of church history. Otto of Freising (died 1158) predicted the thousand years of Satan's bondage would be followed by the final forty-two months of world history, culminating in the overthrow of the Antichrist.[4]

John Wycliffe (1329–1384), often called the "Morning Star" of the Reformation, was extremely popular with the Puritans because he clearly identified the Catholic pope as the Antichrist in his infamous work *De Papa*, published in 1379. He wrote: "The Pope is Antichrist heere in erth, for he is agens [against] Christ both in life and in lore."[5] Thus Wycliffe has come to be viewed as the father of the Protestant apocalyptic tradition.

At the time of the Reformation, Martin Luther (1483–1546) was strongly influenced by Wycliffe's works, concluding that the pope was "the real Antichrist of whom all the Scripture speaks" in his *On the Papacy at Rome*. In 1529, amidst his struggles with both the Roman Catholics and the radical Protestants, Luther discovered a late fifteenth-century commentary on the Apocalypse by John Hilten, a Franciscan monk who identified the Turks with Magog and predicted an invasion of Germany by the Turks—a prospect which seemed a very real possibility in Luther's day. Interestingly, Hilten had also predicted that about 1516 a man would rise up, reform the church, and overthrow the papacy! Luther could not have helped being impressed by such a prediction. By November of that year, Luther identified Gog as the Turks and Magog as the pope.[6]

John Calvin (1509–1564) is considered by many the greatest of the reformers. His *Institutes of the Christian Religion* (1536) were the first great theological works of the Reformation. He also wrote twenty-three commentaries and hundreds of letters, preached almost daily, and set up a Protestant haven at Geneva, Switzerland. He exerted considerable influence over John Knox, the Puritan exiles at Geneva, and on the Duke of Somerset, Protector of England during the reign of Edward VI.

3.   Much more cautious than Luther in eschatology, Calvin deliberately avoided writing a commentary on Revelation. But in his commentary on Thessalonians, he wrote: "The day of Christ will not come until the world has fallen into apostasy, and the rule of the Antichrist has held sway in the Church." He viewed the Antichrist not as the emperor, nor a single pope, but as a succession of popes, stating, "All the marks by which the Spirit of God has pointed out antichrist appear clearly in the pope."[7]

4.   John Bale (1495–1563), bishop, scholar, and an English dramatist, wrote a commentary on the Apocalypse, entitled *The Image of Both Churches*.[8] He viewed the "woman in the wilderness" as the true church and the "whore of Babylon" as the Roman Catholic Church. He was also the first known writer to suggest there were seven periods of time covering the seven dispensations of human history. His importance in the history of dispensational thought has been almost entirely overlooked.

EVEN THE PURITANS COULDN'T GET IT STRAIGHT

Most of the reformers, like John Foxe (1516–1587) who wrote *Foxes Book of Martyrs* (originally, *Actes and Monu-*

ments), believed that the Reformation was God's tool to rid England of the "agents of Babylon," namely, the Catholic Church. Foxe's popularity convinced virtually the entire Church of England that the pope was the Antichrist.

By 1560 the exiled Puritans at Geneva, Switzerland published the first annotated study Bible, known as the Geneva Bible. Having been exiled by the pro-Catholic "Bloody" Mary Tudor, their notes depicted the pope as the Antichrist and the locusts from the bottomless pit as his agents: monks, friars, cardinals, patriarchs, and bishops. The Geneva Bible went through 140 printings and held popular sway over Protestant England even long after the *King James Version* appeared. Like many works at that time, it identified Babylon as symbolizing the Catholic Church and Magog (Ezekiel 38–39) as the Turks and Saracens.

The famous explorer Sir Walter Raleigh (1552–1618), who overwhelmingly defeated the Spanish Armada in 1588, was a favorite of Queen Elizabeth I but fell into disfavor with King James, who imprisoned him in the Tower of London for thirteen years. There he wrote his famous *History of the World*. He dated Creation at 4031 B.C. and divided history into three parts: before the Law, under the Law, and under grace. His views of prophecy led him to identify Magog as the Turks in the East and the Spaniards, "descendants of the Magogonians," in the West. He also pictured Mohammed as the "false prophet" of Revelation.[9]

One of the most far-reaching predictions of the Puritan era was made by Hugh Broughton (1549–1612), who dated Creation at 3926 B.C. and added 6,000 years of human history, culminating in the return of Christ in A.D. 2072![10] Needless to say, Broughton's view was not very popular because it put the Second Coming too far in the then-distant future.

RISE OF MATHEMATICAL CALCULATIONS

One of the most influential Puritan apocalyptists was John Napier (1550–1617) of Merchiston, Scotland.[11] He was recognized as one of the great minds of his day and is still remembered for the invention of logarithms in mathematics. He used his mathematical genius to fill his commentary on Revelation with maps, charts, and chronological tables. Ironically, his mathematical genius led to excessive prophetic speculation as he tried to uncover the mathematical framework of prophecy. Assuming Daniel's prophecy of "seventy weeks" (Daniel 9) is 490 years and then dividing in half, Napier surmised that every 245 years was significant in the rise and fall of empires.

Assuming that the trumpets and bowls of Revelation were synonymous, Napier speculated that the fifth trumpet, "the star that fell," was Mohammed and the fifth vial, the "plague of locusts," was the rise of the Turks, which he dated at A.D. 1051, following Foxe's date. Working backward and forward from 1051, Napier devised this scheme based on 245-year intervals:

Trumpet & Vial	Event	Date
1	Destruction of Jerusalem	71
2	Eastern Empire Established	316
3	Totila Burns Rome	561
4	Charlemagne Becomes Emperor	806
5	Turks Rise Under Zadok	1051
6	Osman	1296
7	Reformation	1541

On the basis of his calculation, Napier said, "The last trumpet and vial beginneth *anno Christi* 1541 and should end in *anno Christi* 1786." He also predicted that 1639 would co-incide with the third angel and usher in the final conflict be-tween Christ (reformers) and Antichrist (Rome). He saw the fourth angel as Christ Himself, whom he predicted would re-turn in 1688 and begin a harvest of the elect until 1786. He was also the first to suggest that the number of the Anti-christ, 666, could be found in the value of the Greek letters spelling *Lateinos,* which he associated with the Roman Cath-olic Church.

Napier's commentary was so popular it was published three times in Edinburgh (1593, 1611, 1645), twice in Lon-don (1594, 1611), twice in Dutch, five times in French, and three times in German. It was later abridged and reissued as *The Bloody Almanack* (1643 and 1647), which became the most powerful apocalyptic literature of the English Civil War, convincing Oliver Cromwell's followers that the final apocalypse had already begun and that they had put the Anti-christ to flight.

THE DATING GAME

From the first appearance of Napier's commentary, the pro-phetic dating game got into full swing. Napier was a mathe-matical genius and lent credibility to such enterprise. Soon Robert Pont (1524–1606), John Knox's son-in-law, tried to relate prophecy to astronomy in his chronological work, *A newe treatise on the right reckoning of the yeares and ages of the world,* which appeared in 1599. He was the first reformer to suggest that six millennia (6,000 years) of human history would be followed by a seventh millennium of peace on earth. Interested in the stars, he speculated that the comet of 1572 was a sign from the Lord, like the star of Bethlehem, heralding the end of the age, and that the eclipse of 1598 had ushered in the final darkness of the end times.

Thomas Brightman (1557–1607) was a Puritan pastor and scholar. His *Revelation of the Revelation,* published in 1609 after his death, became the most popular prophetic tract of Puritan England.[12] Brightman paralleled the seven churches of Revelation 2–3 to the seven ages of church history, suggesting that their distances from Ephesus paralleled the lengths of their ages. He suggested the following scheme:

Church	*Prophetic Period*
1. Ephesus	Apostles to Constantine
2. Smyrna	Constantine to Gratian (382)
3. Pergamum	382 to 1300
4. Thyatira	1300 to 1520
5. Sardis	German Reformation
6. Philadelphia	Genevan Reformation
7. Laodicea	Church of England

Brightman also introduced the idea of double fulfillments; thus the fifth trumpet referred to both Mohammed in the East and Pope Boniface III in the West. In the East the "locusts" were Saracens, while in the West they were monks and friars. The persecuted woman (Revelation 12) was the persecuted church from 300 to 1300, which was served by four "angels": Wycliffe, Hus, Luther, and Calvin. Brightman followed earlier commentators in believing Satan had been bound a thousand years (300–1300) by Constantine, but had broken his shackles and was determined to destroy the true church by a conspiracy between the pope and the Turks.

Brightman believed that the last great "harvest" was brought about by Luther, the "avenging angel" was Thomas Cromwell, and the "soul under the altar" was the martyred Thomas Cranmer. He pictured the seven vials beginning under Queen Elizabeth I in 1560 with the first blast of the seventh trumpet. He offered the following scheme:

Vial One	(1563)	Elizabeth dismissed papal clergy.
Vial Two	(1564)	Council of Trent confirmed the damnation of nonelect.
Vial Three	(1581)	Act of Parliament against papists.
Vial Four	(present)	"boiling heat of the sun is now every day to be looked for . . . whereby the man of sin may be vehemently scorched."
Vial Five	(by 1650)	Fall of Rome (pope).
Vial Six	(future)	Conversion of the Jews.
Vial Seven	(no later than 1695)	Battle of Armageddon.

MILLENNIAL EXPECTATION

Puritan England's leading premillennialist was Joseph Mede (1586–1638).[13] He was one of the outstanding intellectuals of his day, combining the skills of a theologian, linguist, historian, and mathematician. A professor of Greek at Cambridge, Mede wrote an extensive commentary, *The Key to Revelation* (1627) and a shorter work, *The Apostasy of the Latter Times,* which appeared posthumously in 1642. In his works he surmised that the 1,260 days, 42 months, and 3½ years of Revelation all referred to the same time period, which he took to mean 1,260 prophetic years. Rejecting the idea that Satan was bound by Constantine's legitimization of the church, Mede argued that Constantine's legalization of Christianity destroyed its original purity and ushered in an era of 1,260 years of apostasy from A.D. 395 to 1655. He predicted the fall of the Beast (Roman Church) in 1655, after which the "woman" (church) would return from the wilderness to take her proper place in the millennial reign of Christ.

In many ways Mede was the forerunner of later dispensational eschatology. He believed in the literal return of Christ, a thousand-year reign of peace on earth, two judgments separated by the thousand years and the reign of the bride of Christ during the Millennium. He differed with later dispensationalists on the unique position of the church, not Israel, during the Millennium, but he did believe in the future conversion of the Jews, who would evangelize the world and rebuke the Church of Rome for its paganism.

Mede's influence was incredible. Like Napier before him, he brought intellectual authority to the study of prophecy. He taught such great men as John Milton, Isaac Newton, Jeremiah Burroughs, and Nathaniel Holmes. He also influenced the Puritan Thomas Goodwin, who succeeded him as England's leading premillennialist. Mede also corresponded extensively with Bishop James Ussher, whose chronology of dates was included in the original *Scofield Reference Bible* (1909).

As millennial expectation rose, so did militant Puritanism. Thomas Goodwin (1600–1680) and Jeremiah Burroughs (1559–1646) were nonconformist Congregationalists who advocated the literal interpretation of prophetic passages.[14] Suffering persecution under Archbishop William Laud of Canterbury, they radicalized the Puritan view of prophecy calling for the expulsion of King Charles I and Archbishop Laud as agents of the Antichrist. Viewing themselves as the faithful witnesses of the Last Days, they called for the expulsion of Antichrist from the Church of England. Playing off the number 666, Goodwin argued that the Antichrist's power would reach its peak in 1666, to be followed by the fall of the papacy and the Turkish Empire before 1700.

For most of the Puritans, millennial dawn seemed just around the corner with the outbreak of the English Civil War in 1642. The Westminster Assembly convened to rewrite Anglican theology in 1643; Archbishop Laud was executed for treason in 1645; and Charles I was executed as well in 1649. Even the great Puritan scholar John Owen could not resist calling his execution a fulfillment of prophecy in his sermon to Parliament the next day.[15] The British "moral majority" was in full control of England's destiny. But it was not long until the Puritans began arguing among themselves and calling each other the Antichrist, and their movement collapsed. Cromwell died in 1658 and the monarchy was restored in 1660. By 1662 the Act of Uniformity ejected more than 2,000 Puritan pastors from their pulpits and millennial expectation crashed into the bitter reality of political defeat.

Prophetic speculation continued during the eighteenth century, as any reading of Jonathan Edwards' *History of Redemption* will reveal, but it took a milder turn, and many of the old Puritan works went out of print—forever!

In the meantime, Pierre Poiret (1646–1719), a French philosopher, wrote about the seven dispensations in his *L'O Economie Divine*, published in Amsterdam in 1687 and translated into English in 1713. In 1699 John Edwards published *A Complete History or Survey of All the Dispensations* and the hymn writer and theologian Isaac Watts (1674–1748) laid out seven dispensations in his essay entitled, "The Harmony of all the Religions Which God Ever Prescribed to Men and All His Dispensations Towards Them."[16] But it was not until the writings of John Nelson Darby (1800–1882) and the Plymouth Brethren in England, in the nineteenth century, that prophetic expectation would reach a new crescendo.

THE PLYMOUTH BRETHREN

Darby had left the Church of England because of his strong personal commitment to the Scriptures and joined a group of "Brethren" in the winter of 1827–1828 at Dublin, Ireland. They were a simple group of believers who broke bread every Lord's Day and believed in the liberty of ministry as a calling of God and not the ordination of man. He later moved to Plymouth, England in 1831, where his teachings about Bible prophecy flourished. Followers included such prominent men as George Müller of Bristol and numerous biblical scholars like George Wigram and Samuel Tregelles.[17]

Darby and the other Plymouth Brethren adopted a scheme of seven dispensations of God's economy in human history that were similar to those of Isaac Watts:

1. Paradise to the Flood
2. Noah to Abraham
3. Abraham to Moses
4. Israel
5. Gentiles
6. The Spirit
7. The Millennium[18]

Unique to the teachings of Darby and the Brethren was the emphasis on the pre-Tribulation Rapture of the church. They believed that Christ would come to Rapture ("translate") His bride, the true church, out of the world before the Tribulation Period began. Thus, the pre-Tribulation Rapture became a cornerstone to their eschatology which viewed the Tribulation as a time of divine judgment necessary to bring about the conversion of the Jews and the downfall of the Antichrist.

Darby's teaching greatly influenced others like W.E. Blackstone, whose popular book *Jesus Is Coming* was published in 1878; and G. Campbell Morgan (1864–1945), who became one of England's greatest dispensational pastors and authors; and evangelist Dwight L. Moody of Chicago, who touched the world with his preaching. Their combined influence was also felt in the Bible conference movement of the nineteenth century where many of the prophetic themes that influence the evangelical church today were developed.[19] In time, other dispensational teachers rose to prominence like A.J. Gordon of Boston and James H. Brookes of St. Louis.

LAODICEAN LIBERALS

While dispensationalists emphasized the imminent return of Christ to rapture the church at any moment, they were generally careful not to set any dates. However, it was common among dispensationalists to view the seven churches of Revelation as predicting the seven ages of church history in the following manner:[20]

1. Ephesus   Apostolic Age, 30–100
2. Smyrna   Persecuted church, 100–300
3. Pergamum   Roman Church, 300–1200
4. Thyatira   Medieval church, 1200–1500
5. Sardis   Reformation church, 1500–1700
6. Philadelphia   Missionary church, 1700–1900
7. Laodicea   Apostate church, 1900–?

While no dates were set for the second coming of Christ in this scheme, the very fact that prophecy preachers paralleled Laodicea to the rise of theological liberalism in the mainline churches created the impression that the church stood at the end of the Church Age and apostasy was already at work. The popularity of this idea was spread by enormous reception given to C.I. Scofield's (1843–1921) *Scofield Reference*

Bible, originally published in 1909. Like many of the Puritans and Plymouth Brethren before them, America's twentieth-century premillennialists eagerly look forward in anticipation to the second coming of Christ to set up His kingdom on earth.

CULTIC CONFUSION

All of this is quite remarkable in light of some of the classic millenarian schemes which tragically failed. In the 1820s Joseph Smith, founder of the Mormons, claimed to have been visited by an angel named Moroni, who directed him to discover and translate the golden tablets of the *Book of Mormon,* which was first published in 1830. That same year the "Church of Jesus Christ of Latter Day Saints" was officially organized. Smith's followers believed they were living in the Last Days when Christ would return to set up His millennial kingdom on earth for His saints, at Salt Lake City, Utah.

In the meantime, William Miller, a Baptist pastor in Vermont, assumed that the "2,300 days" from the transgression of the sanctuary to the cleansing of the sanctuary, mentioned in Daniel 8:14, could be calculated as 2,300 years and could be dated from the proclamation to rebuild the Jerusalem temple in 457 B.C.. By adding 2,300 years he predicted that Christ would return literally in 1843. He later refined the date to October 22, 1844. When the day of "Great Disappointment" came, Miller gave up the whole idea, but many of his followers refused to do so and adopted the idea that on that date Christ moved into the holy of holies in the heavenly temple to begin His atonement for our sins. Thus, the Seventh Day Adventist movement began and has grown to considerable size and influence with its insistence on Saturday (Sabbath) worship in rejection of the "mark of the Beast," which they view as Sunday worship.

Toward the end of the nineteenth century, Charles Russell began to predict the return of Christ to establish His kingdom on earth in 1914. He published voluminously, including *Zion's Watch Tower* magazine and a lengthy series entitled *Millennial Dawn* (later called *Studies in Scripture*). When Christ did not return visibly in 1914, Russell's followers assumed He had returned secretly, revealing Himself only to Jehovah's Witnesses as they called themselves, believing they were the 144,000 faithful witnesses of the Apocalypse. Presuming the Church Age to have ended, they began meeting in "Kingdom Halls" to practice their faith.[21]

VIEWING PROPHECY THROUGH OUR OWN EYES

Perhaps the greatest problem for the church in the matter of interpreting biblical prophecy is the desire to view it through our own experience. The German theologians call this a *zeitgeist,* a current mood or response to certain existing conditions.[22] Unfortunately, as we have seen in this brief history of eschatological speculation, this has happened more often than not. The great temptation in prophetic interpretation is to move from the facts to our own *assumptions* and *speculations.*

The twentieth century is loaded with examples of prophetic speculations which never came true. First, it was *assumed* that ours must be the last age and that in the last days the Antichrist will form an alliance of European nations and attack Israel. Here is just a sample of the proposals that were offered:

1. *Kaiser Wilhelm*
   The German emperor's title meant "Càesar," and he

intended to conquer all of Europe and reunite the old Roman Empire. Even the popular American evangelist Billy Sunday bought this idea, often stating: "If you turn hell upside down, you'll find 'made in Germany' stamped on the bottom!" During World War I, the Kaiser was the most likely candidate for the Antichrist.

2. *Benito Mussolini*

The Italian strongman from Rome rose to power in Europe after World War I, and prophetic speculators tagged him as the Antichrist long before World War II began. After all, they reasoned, Mussolini is in Rome and wants to revive the Roman Empire; therefore, he will join hands with the people and rule the world.

3. *Adolph Hitler*

Hitler has come to be the ultimate personification of evil. What better candidate for the Antichrist? He persecuted and murdered 6 million Jews and tried to conquer all of Europe. He formed a murderous alliance with Mussolini and turned his hand against everyone, but alas, they were both destroyed.

4. *Joseph Stalin*

This atheistic leader of the Soviet Union may have been our ally during World War II, but it was an uneasy alliance at best. Some American prophecy buffs had him tagged as the "Man of Sin" long before and after Hitler. After all, they suggested, Russia is the Magog of Ezekiel's prophecy (Ezekiel 38–39).

5. *Nikita Khrushchev*

Many still remember the outspoken, shoe-pounding, bald, fat man of the Soviet Union from his violent speech at the United Nations in which he threatened to bury us all. Surely, he could be the Antichrist. Right? Nope!

6. *Gamal Abdel Nasser*

In 1956 the leader of Egypt defied the Western powers and invaded Israel, only to suffer a humiliating defeat when the U.S. and the British intervened. Some saw him as a candidate for the final persecutor of Israel.

7. *John F. Kennedy*

Believe it or not—he was a top candidate among anti-Catholic fundamentalists in the early 1960s. They were sure he was going to deceive the world and form an alliance with the pope, the blacks, and the communists to take over the world.

8. *Mikhail Gorbachev*

Recent evangelicals have been very nervous about Gorbachev. He seems too good to be true with his *perestroika* and *glasnost* offers of peace, while holding the balance of power in check with his nuclear arsenal. I have even had people ask me if the mark on his head might be the "mark of the Beast!"

9. *Ronald Wilson Reagan*

Yes, even the darling of the New Right and practically the entire evangelical church was targeted as a candidate for Antichrist because his three names each contain six letters, thus 666.

10. *Saddam Hussein*

How could he possibly be the Antichrist? Some are already suggesting he will sign a peace treaty with Israel only to break it later and renew his hostilities toward the Promised Land.

Other candidates have included Henry Kissinger, Margaret Thatcher, and of course, George Bush! The problem with these identifications is that they are always tentative and viewed through the *zeitgeist* of our own times. Identifications which now seem ludicrous once held great popular appeal.

The real tragedy is that instead of rejecting prophetic speculation for what it is, we are often duped by it. People guessing dates and selecting candidates for the Antichrist are claiming to know more than the writers of Scripture, and that is always dangerous. Dr. Daniel Mitchell writes: "Speculating on the date of Christ's return not only breeds bad theology, but it is the original sin all over again—trying to know as much as God."[23] He goes on to note that the expectation of Christ's return *at any moment* has been a source of hope and comfort to the church since the days of the apostles. Any apparent delay is not due to God's indecision, but to the fact that He has not let us in on the secret!

I believe the Bible clearly predicts the rise of a personal Antichrist at the end of human history, but I doubt we will ever know who he is until it is too late. The Apostle Paul said of him, "Don't let anyone deceive you in any way, for that day will not come until the rebellion occurs and the man of lawlessness ["man of sin," KJV] is revealed, the man doomed to destruction" (2 Thessalonians 2:3). Paul reminds us that the "power of lawlessness" (2 Thessalonians 2:7) is already at work, but it will eventually culminate when the lawless one is revealed (2 Thessalonians 2:8).

In the meantime, we are admonished to "stand firm" and hold to the doctrine of the apostles of our Lord (2 Thessalonians 2:15) that we might be strengthened "in every good deed and word" (2 Thessalonians 2:17). Thus, Paul's advice to us is the same as that of the Lord Jesus who told us to watch, stay ready, and keep serving until He comes (Matthew 24:42-46).

When you study the *facts* of prophecy, be sure that you distinguish them from the *assumptions* you draw or the *speculations* you make. While we would all like to believe that our Lord will come in our lifetime, it is presumption to assume that we are the terminal generation. Surely, He could come today, but He may not come for many years. That decision is up to God the Father.

5

THE
GATHERING
STORM

Darkness was already falling in Chicago at 3:36 P.M. on December 2, 1942, when a group of scientists huddled together on the dimly lit squash court of The University of Chicago's abandoned football stadium. Following a technique used in 1939 by German scientists who had succeeded in splitting the atom, they produced the first controlled nuclear fission chain reaction in history. Less then three years later, their discovery would lead to the most dreadful weapon in human history—the atomic bomb.

In a desert expanse 50 miles from Alamogordo, New Mexico, the first atomic bomb was exploded at 5:20 A.M. July 16, 1945. Then, less than three weeks later, President Harry Truman gave the orders to drop an atomic bomb on Hiroshima, Japan at 8:15 A.M. on August 6. It leveled two-thirds of the city of 350,000 people in the most incredible decimation in human history.

By 1949 the Soviet Union had also developed the atomic bomb, and the Cold War was under way. Then, on November 1, 1952 the United States tested the first hydrogen bomb on a small atoll in the Pacific Ocean. The explosion was so devastating that it blew the one-mile island of Elugelab right out of the Pacific, leaving a 175-foot-deep hole in its place in the ocean floor! A frightening new era of apocalyptic proportions had dawned.

LIVING WITH
THE BOMB

Despite all the miscalculations of the past, many people believe that the storm clouds are gathering on the horizon of humanity today. Ours is a very different world from any that has ever preceded it. On February 7, 1991, Army General Colin Powell, Chairman of the Joint Chiefs of Staff for the United States Armed Forces, warned: "The Soviet Union still remains the one country in the world that could destroy us in thirty minutes!"[1] For the first time in history, it is possible to destroy the entire world with nuclear weapons in one hour.

While the desire for peace clings to the deepest crevice of the human heart, the prospects for global destruction are greater ultimately than the prospects for global peace. Undoubtedly, the present crisis will result in some attempted settlement and peaceful solution. But beyond the coming peace is the final holocaust.

Sir Winston Churchill said that in the twentieth century, "War began to enter into its kingdom as the potential destroyer of the human race." Today the vast coalition of nations and the modern weapons of warfare are such that the enterprise of slaughter can be, as Churchill put it, "executed on a scale and with a perseverance never before imagined."[2]

PSYCHOLOGICAL EFFECTS OF A
WORLD GONE MAD

Since 1945, when the atomic bomb was dropped on Hiroshima, Japan, mankind has lived with the threat of nuclear annihilation. The "baby boomers," those born in the population boom after World War II, could just as easily be called the generation of the bomb. Many psychologists believe that people in this generation do not think like any generation that has ever preceded them because they have to live with the reality of their own vulnerability every day.

Educator Arthur Levine has described the current mentality as, "Going first class on the Titanic!"[3] In his study sponsored by the Carnegie Foundation for the Advancement of Teaching, Levine found that today's students are self-centered, individualistic "escapists" who want little responsibility for solving society's problems, but who want society to provide them with the opportunity to fulfill their pleasures. They have given up noble causes because they have given up any real hope of solving the world's problems. They see themselves on a hopeless voyage destined to disaster. Unable to turn the ship around, they simply clamor for the first-class seats so they can enjoy the ride until the inevitable strikes.

It should not surprise us, therefore, that people today will spare almost no expense for elaborate vacations, expensive trips, and romantic cruises. They are trying to pretend everything is all right, even though they know it isn't.

PROLIFERATION OF
NUCLEAR WEAPONS

The Center for Defense Information estimates that the United States alone has an arsenal of over 35,000 nuclear weapons and is capable of producing them at the rate of 3 per day. Each of these bombs carries the equivalent of 460 million tons of TNT—35,000 times *greater* than the atomic bomb that killed 70,000 people at Hiroshima in 1945.

The Soviet Union's 100-megaton H-bombs are each capable of creating an all-consuming fire storm 170 miles in diameter. Just 18–20 of these superbombs could destroy 75 percent of the population of the United States in less than 1 hour! American retaliation includes enough nuclear warheads to wipe out 400 million people in the Soviet Union and China within 30 minutes' time.[4]

Today the United States, Great Britain, France, the USSR, China, and India already have atomic weapons. Israel, South Africa, and Germany likely have the bomb as well. And how soon till almost any well-funded dictator in the oil-rich Middle East will have nuclear warheads at his disposal? As the clock of time ticks on, it is only a matter of time until the inevitable disaster strikes.

THE FINAL BLAST

The Bible predicts the final devastation of the earth in "one hour" (Revelation 18:10) of the destruction of the prophetic "Babylon," the symbolic name for the kingdom of the Antichrist. The Bible says, "All your riches and splendor have vanished, never to be recovered" (Revelation 18:14). Even the merchants and sailors will not come near this land, but will "stand far off, terrified at her torment," and crying out: "In one hour such great wealth has been brought to ruin!" (Revelation 18:15, 17)

The Apostle Peter provides an even more vivid description of the final blast that shall devastate this planet when he warns: "But the Day of the Lord will come like a thief. The heavens will disappear with a roar; the elements will be destroyed by fire, and the earth and everything in it will be laid bare" (2 Peter 3:10).

John Phillips notes that Peter's prophecy of a great end-times conflagration of the earth and its atmosphere uses precise terminology which accurately describe a nuclear explosion. The "elements" (Greek, *stoicheia*) are defined by Liddell and Scott's *Lexicon* as "the components into which matter is divided" (or atoms) and the term "dissolved" (Greek, *luo*) comes from the basic Greek word meaning to "loose" that which is bound (as in nuclear fission). The term "great noise" (Greek, *rhoizedon*) is found nowhere else in the New Testament and signifies "a rushing sound as of roaring flames." The term "fervent heat" is derived from the Greek medical term *kausoo*, denoting a fever. But Peter's use of it in application to inanimate objects is the only such known usage anywhere in Greek literature. Thus, Phillips concludes, "Peter described in accurate terms the untying of the atom and the resulting rushing, fiery destruction which follows it."[5] "That day will bring about the destruction of the heavens by fire, and the elements will melt" (2 Peter 3:12).

DETERIORATION OF EARTH'S RESOURCES

The great oil spill in the Persian Gulf was one more in a series of ecological disasters in humanity's war against the earth, which *Time* magazine called "eco-war."[6] The environmental carnage in the Gulf War resulted in burning oil refineries, bombed out chemical plants, and the largest crude oil petroleum dump in the history of the world. As Iraqi troops set Kuwait's oil refineries ablaze, they also apparently dumped millions of gallons of crude oil into the shallow waters of the Persian Gulf at Kuwait's supertanker loading pier, the Sea Island Terminal.

Ecological experts have called it the worst environmental damage ever done to the earth. Because of the enclosed nature of the Persian Gulf, whose only outlet to the sea is the thirty-five-mile-wide Strait of Hormuz, the gulf is especially vulnerable to ecological warfare. Hussein's cruel attack on the environment turned the "mother of all battles" against the earth in a perverse act of environmental terrorism.

But the deterioration of the earth's resources goes far beyond a giant oil spill. Air pollution is so bad in many of the earth's industrial cities that it is becoming a major problem for future survival. The gradual evaporation of the ozone layer could result in more severe forms of skin cancer than have ever been known before. Radiation leaks, like the one at Chernobyl in the Soviet Union, could spell major disaster for the inhabitants of earth.

Interestingly, biblical prophecy declares that God's judgment will include "destroying them which destroy the earth" (Revelation 11:18). Dave Hunt observes, "A number of God's judgments are ecological in nature, devastating the grass and trees and polluting oceans and rivers."[7] The Bible predicts a terrible ecological disaster in the last days of the Great Tribulation before the Christ returns to spare the world from total destruction.

MISMANAGEMENT OF THE NATURAL ENVIRONMENT

The oil war in the Middle East reminded us all of the continuing problems of our mismanagement of the natural environment. Lack of strategic oil reserves and the continued gluttonous consumption of oil by the industrial giants will eventually deplete our supply. But again, the ecological problems facing us and our children are much greater than the oil crisis.

The destruction of the Amazon rain forests has been called "one of the great tragedies of history."[8] What is at stake in the Amazon is the greatest supply of oxygen in the whole world. Now years of assault by builders, developers, and settlers have endangered the supply. Philip Fearnside of Brazil's National Institute for Research in the Amazon says, "Unless things change, the forest *will* disappear."

Third World countries need their resources for their own economic growth and development. But when this need turns to environmental rape, everyone loses. One need only consider places like Haiti, where greedy men have stripped away the natural resources and left an environmental catastrophe in their selfish path.

Biblical prophecy points to the end of the world when the natural environment of the earth is devastated. The seas and rivers of earth are described as "blood . . . every living thing in the sea died" (Revelation 16:3). The air is depicted as so thick that no one can see the sun, and yet people are "seared by the intense heat" (Revelation 16:9). While we can only *assume* what this will mean, it certainly sounds like the aftereffects of a disastrous nuclear war.

EXPLODING GLOBAL ECONOMY

In recent months it has become abundantly clear that the global economy is fast replacing individual national economies. What happens on the stock market in Tokyo early in the day dominoes in its effect on the trading floors of London and New York later in the same day. With the instantaneous communication systems of telephones, fax, computers, and even satellite telecasts, the world is now at our doorstep. Economic isolation is a thing of the past.

Economic cooperation is becoming the name of the game in Europe. In 1992 the continent-wide deregulatory movement kicks into high gear, forming the New Europe. The twelve members of the European Economic Community (EEC) have removed most of the trade barriers and internal regulations that have separated their countries for centuries. The end result will be a European passport and driver's license valid in all EEC nations. This will spur international travel on the continent where an invigorated European market with the free flow of money, goods, services, and workers has the potential to become the world's economic giant.

The EEC headquarters in Brussels, Belgium is the central nervous system of the New Europe, whose motto is: "Many Tongues, One Voice." For the first time since the sixteenth century and the Holy Roman Empire of Charles V, Europe now stands ready to unite again. *Europe* magazine interestingly reported that the basic silver coins of the European currency unit will have twelve stars and a bust of Charles V imprinted on them.[9]

The EEC had its beginnings in the democratic alliance of Belgium, the Netherlands, Luxembourg, Italy, France, and West Germany. By 1973 it also included Denmark, Ireland, and Great Britain. Greece joined in 1981, and Spain and Portugal brought the membership total to twelve in 1986. Now the reunification of East and West Germany makes Germany the dominant player in the EEC. And the democratization of the formerly communist nations of Eastern Europe opens vast potential for the growth of the European giant. Jean Monnet, the original architect of the EEC, said that the economic community itself was "only a stage on the way to the organized world of tomorrow."[10]

A unified political federation in Europe seemed like an impossible dream in 1957, but now it appears to be a future reality. Even powerful Margaret Thatcher was swept out of office for resisting the tide of popular support for the EEC. One can only *speculate* whether this has anything to do with the prophecies of a global economy in the last days. The Apocalypse tells us that "no one could buy or sell unless he had the mark, which is the name of the Beast or the number of his name" (Revelation 13:17). Whatever the mark of the Beast is, this passage implies that no financial transactions will occur without it.

We can only *speculate* how this will come about. Years ago, prophetic writers depicted people with numbers branded on their heads or hands. Today, prophetic writers speculate that these may be "invisible" computer codes indelibly "tattooed" on the body for computer identification. There is nothing wrong with such speculation if it is healthy, creative, and helpful—and if we don't preach it as *fact.* The Bible does not mention computers per se, but it now seems reasonable that they may be in view here. However, twenty years from now something else even may have taken their place; technology races ahead faster than we realize.

For instance, several years ago I picked up Delta Airlines' *Sky* magazine and read a fascinating article entitled, "Electronic Money Will Change Your Life."[11] In the article, the author explained that one day every bank in America would be linked up to the same central computer and that "electronic funds transfer systems" would eventually lead to a "cashless society" dependent on "paperless transactions." He talked about credit and debit charges for the purchase of merchandise at point of sale terminals and the automatic deduction of monthly payments from one's bank account.

It seemed rather farfetched at the time. Even the author admitted it would take the general public time to get used to this concept. He suggested that "1995 is a fair guess." My how time flies!

THE ISLAMIC CURTAIN

In an age of secularism and pseudo-religions, the beliefs and prejudices of Islam remain deeply entrenched. It is often pictured as a religion of fanatics, terrorists, and warmongers. While this is not a fair picture of Islam on the whole, it is, nevertheless, true of a radical element within the Muslim faith. This radical element causes most Westerners to be repulsed by Islamic concepts of justice, revenge, and so-called "holy wars."

The "Islamic Curtain" cuts off the Arab world from outside influences. "Behind that wall of prejudice," Hunt observes, "any religion except Islam is forbidden."[12] Political leaders see themselves as protectors of Islam. Converts to Christianity are often persecuted, imprisoned, and even executed. In many Islamic countries, Christians have been put to death by their own families! Gospel preaching is outlawed and Gospel literature is banned from public distribution. Freedom of the press, of speech, and of public assembly is forbidden.

Some authors suggest that international pressure and exposure to the West through radio and television may wear down the Islamic Curtain one day. I do not feel that is very likely. A morally bankrupt system of atheistic communism is more likely to collapse than a deeply entrenched religious faith, false though it may be.

The Koran, the sacred book of Islam, advocates the killing of apostates and unbelievers. Muhammad himself led several battles, claiming that God had called him to spread Islam with the point of the sword. History tells us that Muhammad's followers swept across the Middle East and North Africa conquering everyone in their path. They crossed into Europe and took Spain, but they were finally turned back by Charles Martel in the Battle of Tours in France in A.D. 732. Even today it is considered an honorable duty for Muslims to kill Christians and Jews.

Hunt is correct when he writes: "It is impossible to understand the current situation in the Middle East, much less anticipate probable future developments there, except in the context of the religion that grips and motivates the Arab world."[13] This is a world of diverse peoples held together by the bond of a common religion, Islam, and a common language, Arabic. Together, these elements have a vice-like grip on the Muslim world.

This is not to say that the Arab world has not made significant contributions to the world in art, literature, architecture, mathematics, and science. The intricate geometric designs of Islamic art are among the most beautiful in the world. The Arab people themselves can be kind, loving, and hospitable. We must be careful not to close the door of the Gospel to them by failing to love them for the sake of Christ. But when it comes to religion, there is something demonic about their hatred of Jews and Christians.

THE LAST JIHAD

Tragically, the Prophet Ezekiel predicts an invasion of Israel in the "Last Days" by a host of Arab nations (Ezekiel 38–39). This prophecy was given centuries before the rise of Islam, and yet it names Persia (Iran), Cush (Sudan/Ethiopia), and Put (Libya) as part of the invading force along with Gomer (Cimmerians from the Russian steppes) and Beth Togarmah "from the far north" (Turkey).[14]

This alliance is headed by Gog, the "chief prince" of Magog. Much has been said about the identification of Magog. The ancient Jewish historian Josephus (*Antiquities*, 1.123) identified them by the Greek term "Scythians" (barbarians from the northern frontiers). Alfonso III of Spain (A.D. 866–910) interpreted Ezekiel's prophecy as depicting the defeat of the Moors (Muslims) in Spain. Others have seen them as Huns, Mongols, Magyars, Turks, and Russians.

The *Scofield Reference Bible* (1909) stated that Magog was Russia, and the communist revolution of 1917 helped that identification to stick in popular evangelical circles. It must be carefully admitted, however, that Scofield's identifications were based on limited records available to nineteenth-century scholars like Keil and Delitzsch. While they are similar to more-recently discovered records, they are not identical. Magog may well designate the barbaric hordes from Southern Russia, but this is an *assumption* based on limited *facts*. Other identifications in the text, such as "chief prince" (Hebrew, *rosh*) being the root word for Russia, Meshech being Moscow, Tubal being Tobolsk, and Gomer being Germany, are almost totally rejected by modern scholars and linguists.

Here is a case in point for distinguishing the *facts* of prophecy from the *assumptions* and *speculations* drawn from them.

Fact. Magog, Persia, Cush, Put, Gomer, and Togarmah will invade Israel "in the Last Days" and be destroyed (Ezekiel 38–39).

Assumption. We can identify these ancient peoples as modern Russia, Iran, Sudan/Ethiopia, Libya, and Turkey.

Speculation. Russia and her Arab allies will invade Israel during the Tribulation Period and be destroyed. Even a careful scholar as Walvoord states this as though it were fact.[15]

Yet there is nothing in the Ezekiel passage about the Tribulation Period. This is generally *assumed* because the invasion described in Ezekiel 38–39 follows the prediction of the regathering of Israel in Ezekiel 37.

Meshech (*Muski*) and Tubal (*Tabal*) are also mentioned in Ezekiel 32:26 in reference to an alliance with the hordes of Egypt, Assyria, and Elam, but most prophetic commentators do not even refer to this passage as having any future significance.

The Prophet Jeremiah predicts an invasion of Babylon by "Ararat, Minni and Ashkenaz" (Jeremiah 51:27). The name "Ararat" refers to the mountain where Noah's ark rested after the Flood and appears in Isaiah 37:38 and 2 Kings 19:37, as "Armenia" in the KJV, following the Septuagint. Yamauchi notes that the biblical name *Ararat* is cognate with Urartu, the mountainous region north of Assyria which proved to be a formidable rival to the Assyrians in the eighth century B.C.[16] These people settled the region later known as Soviet Armenia. *Ashkenaz* is the Hebrew equivalent of the Akkadian name for the Scythians, *Ishkuza*. The general term "Scythian" designates the nomadic tribes from the Russian steppes.

If Ezekiel's prophecy is about the future, since no such invasion is known biblically or historically, then we can *assume* it will yet happen. That being the case, twentieth-century evangelicals have often assumed that the Bible is predicting a Russian-Arab alliance against Israel in the last days. This may well occur, but it is only an *assumption* at best.

Let me digress for a moment and do some *speculating* of my own. Let us assume Ezekiel is predicting an event which is still in the future, when these nations will form an alliance against Israel. Since we know that Iran, Libya, Turkey, Sudan, and Ethiopia are all Muslim (or Muslim influenced),

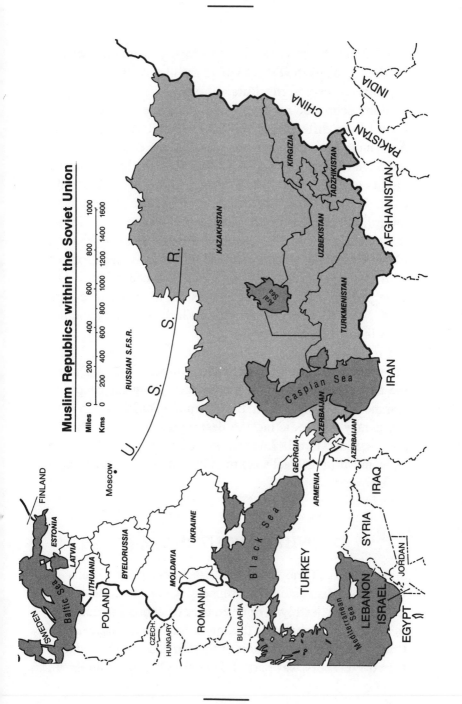

Muslim Republics within the Soviet Union

could it not be possible that the Muslim republics of the southern part of the Soviet Union are in view in this prophecy and not necessarily Russia itself?

Many people do not realize that the Soviet Union is made up of fifteen different republics, of which Russia is only one. Also, most Americans are unaware that one citizen in five in the Soviet Union is Muslim. These Muslims live in the republics of Kazakhstan, Uzbekistan, Turkmenistan, Tadzhikistan, Kirgizia, and Azerbaijan. If the current movement toward independence were to continue in the Soviet Union, these Muslim republics could eventually break away from Moscow. Several Muslim political parties have been formed with this agenda. These Soviet Muslims could join a last great *jihad* ("holy war") against Israel in an alliance with other Muslim states. This could fulfill the prophecy and not even involve Russia!

I make this suggestion based on pure *speculation*. I have never seen this in print by prophetic prognosticators. During the anti-communist era, it was more exciting for people to assume the Bible predicted the destruction of Russia. In reality, it may be predicting the destruction of a last Muslim *jihad* against Israel. Imagine the reaction throughout the Muslim world if Israel were to attempt to rebuild the temple in Jerusalem.

WHAT ABOUT IRAQ?

Strangely, Iraq (Babylon) is not listed among the nations invading Israel in Ezekiel's prophecy. Could this mean that Iraq has been destroyed or taken over by another nation such as Iran? Any answer to this question is pure *speculation*. Prior to the British conquest of the Turks during World War I, Iraq's territory was part of Turkey's Ottoman Empire. In

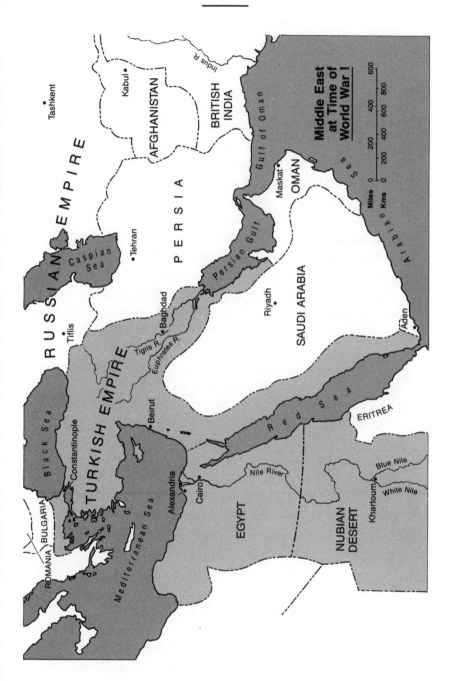

reality, if Iraq could claim it owned Kuwait, Turkey could claim it owns Iraq.

Mesopotamia (Iraq) was conquered by Muslim Arabs in the seventh century A.D. Then under the Abbasid caliphate, Baghdad was made the imperial capital in about A.D. 750. Later, the Seljuk Turks, established dominion over Iraq in A.D. 1055 and continued to be the dominant influence in the area in the following centuries despite brief interludes of Mongol and Persian control.

From the conquest of Suleyman the Magnificent in 1534, until World War I, the Turks had virtual control of the Middle East. In 1914, the British landed at Basra, but were unsuccessful until the archeologist-adventurer, T.E. Lawrence ("Lawrence of Arabia"), persuaded Sharif Hussein of Mecca to revolt against the Turks. Baghdad fell to the British and Saudi forces in 1917. Sharif Hussein later became the King of Saudi Arabia and his son Faisal became King of Iraq in 1921. In 1958, Iraq federated with Jordan, ruled by another descendant of Sharif Hussein. But military revolts led to a series of revolutionary governments that finally resulted in the Arab Socialist Renaissance (Ba'ath) Party coming to power in 1968.

Throughout the Ba'ath control of Iraq there has been a great deal of interest in emphasizing the ancient history of Babylon. Attempts have been made frequently to identify Iraqi sovereignty with the past greatness of ancient Babylon. But it was Saddam Hussein who determined to use this interest to build a monument to himself.

WILL BABYLON BE REBUILT?

Charles Dyer argues that modern Iraq will rebuild the ancient city of Babylon and even offers pictures of the limited reconstruction that was done at the site of the ancient ruins of Babylon under Saddam Hussein's authority.[17] Dyer then *speculates* that Babylon will be rebuilt, become the dominant city in the Middle East, and finally be totally destroyed in fulfillment of the prophecies of Isaiah 13:1-22 and Jeremiah 50:1-42.

While this is certainly possible, it is highly improbable! Biblical scholars have been almost unanimous in their belief that the prophecies of Babylon's fall were fulfilled in ancient times and serve to foreshadow the fall of the symbolic "Babylon" of the future (Revelation 14–18). Gleason Archer writes: "This fall of Babylon is prophetically typical of the overthrow of latter-day Babylon."[18]

Dyer argues that the prophecies of Babylon's fall refer to a violent and total overthrow. "Babylon . . . will be overthrown by God like Sodom and Gomorrah. She will never be inhabited or lived in through all generations" (Isaiah 13:19-20). When Babylon fell to the Medes and Persians in 539 B.C. under Cyrus the Great, it did fall in one night, but it was not a violent destruction. The Prophet Daniel was in Babylon at the time and predicted its overthrow to King Belshazzar (Daniel 5).

THE FALL OF BABYLON

Babylon "fell" (actually, capitulated is a better term) to the Persian army of Cyrus. However, it should be remembered that Cyrus had crossed the Tigris River as early as 547 B.C. and conquered the Kingdom of Lydia, whose capital was Sardis (same as in Revelation 3:1) and whose king was the wealthy Croesus (known to the Greeks as Midas). In the meantime, Cyrus turned south and began sacking the cities of Babylonia, until Babylon itself was cut off and besieged.

Nabonidus the ruler of Babylon fled, leaving Belshazzar, the co-regent in charge. This explains why Belshazzar offered to make Daniel the "third ruler" in the kingdom (Daniel 5:29). Belshazzar himself was only second in command.

Babylon fell the night of the writing on the wall during the drunken festival; this festival is also mentioned by the historians Herodotus and Xenophon. Herodotus also attributed the fall of the city to the Persians' clever diverting of the Euphrates River, permitting the Persian and Median troops to enter the city along the riverbed.[19] Isaiah's reference to the Medes (Isaiah 13:17) and his later prediction of the rise of Cyrus (Isaiah 44–45) have caused most evangelical commentators to assume this prophecy was fulfilled initially in the one-night capture of the city by the Medes and Persians.

Cyrus then appointed a governor, called Darius the Mede in Daniel 5:30, over the city of Babylon. Cyrus himself was killed in battle in 530 B.C. and buried in a tomb that still stands at Pasargadae, the ancient Persian capital. Cyrus was succeeded in turn by Cambyses II (ruled 592–522 B.C.) and Darius the Great (ruled 521–486 B.C.), who extended the borders of the Persian Empire. Darius wintered at Babylon and appointed his son Xerxes (the Ahasuerus who married Esther [Esther 1:1]) as his personal representative in the ancient city. Xerxes later ruled from 485 to 465 B.C. and conducted several expeditions against the Greeks.

It was under Xerxes that Babylon revolted against its Persian overlords, and Xerxes responded harshly in 482 B.C. and attacked the city, demolishing its fortifications and burning the temple of Marduk (god of Babylon) to the ground. Thus, the biblical prophecies were further fulfilled. Babylon still existed, but it was a shell of what it had once been. What influence Esther, a descendant of Jewish captives, may have had on her husband's decision is pure speculation.

ATTEMPTS TO REBUILD

When the Persian Empire finally fell to Alexander the Great of Macedonia in 331 B.C., Alexander resolved to make Babylon his eastern capital. He put 10,000 soldiers to work clearing the debris left by Xerxes and rebuilding some of the structures which had been destroyed. But his disastrous campaigns to Bactria (Afghanistan) and India left him exhausted, and he died in Babylon on his return home on June 13, 323 B.C. After that the fate of Babylon was left to Alexander's generals, the *Diadochi* (successors). With Alexander's death, the plans for rebuilding Babylon died as well. God protected the prophecy from being contradicted.

In 312 B.C. Seleucus captured the remains of the embattled city which had been virtually destroyed by ensuing battles for its control. Unwilling to rebuild the devastated city, Seleucus founded a new city in 305 B.C., named for himself, Seleucia-on-the-Tigris, about ninety kilometers north of Babylon. Eventually the civilian population of Babylon was forced to move there by Seleucus and his successor, Antiochus I (ruled 281–261 B.C.).[20]

During the Hellenistic period, Babylon was reduced to a village, with nearby Esagila maintained as a religious site. One last attempt to rebuild it to its former glory was made by the infamous Antiochus IV Epiphanes, who founded a Greek colony there in 173 B.C., complete with a theater and a gymnasium. Ancient cuneiform texts hail Antiochus as "Founder of the City" and the "Savior of Asia." He was the same ruler who conquered Jerusalem and desecrated the temple during the Intertestamental Period. He appears in biblical prophecy as a type of the Antichrist (Daniel 11:36-45).

In time, the Seleucid kings lost control of Babylon to the Parthians. One of their rulers, Mithradates I, conquered Babylon in 141 B.C. Another, Himerus, destroyed the city and its

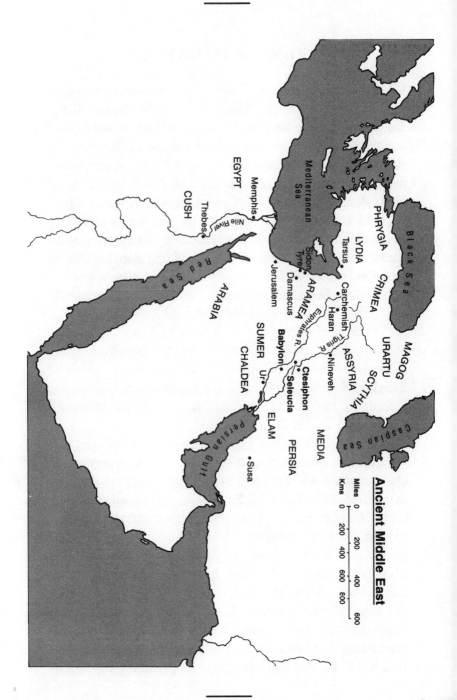

Ancient Middle East

temples in 123 B.C. The Parthians moved their capital to the city of Ctesiphon, across the Tigris from Seleucia, leaving Babylon in ruins. By 24 B.C. Strabo described Babylon as empty and desolate. Though a small Jewish community existed there during Roman times, it was later totally abandoned. When the Roman Emperor Trajan stopped there in A.D. 116, he found nothing but ruins.[21] Left behind was the largest mound of ruins in ancient Mesopotamia (modern Iraq), covering 340 acres. Thus, the name "Babylon," once associated with greatness and splendor, came to refer to a great ruins. The great Babylon had been reduced to rubble! The city that fell in one night eventually decayed into the sands of time. The Hebrew prophets were right and their predictions were fulfilled.

WILL BABYLON RISE AGAIN?

Those who have predicted the rise of Babylon in the end times point out that the prophets predicted Babylon's walls and towers would be torn down (Jeremiah 50:15; 51:30), that Babylon "will never be inhabited" (Isaiah 13:20), and even her stones will be left untouched (Jeremiah 51:26). Dyer argues that small populations have been found near Babylon at various times since the Middle Ages. He also notes that German archeologist Robert Koldewey found people quarrying the city's ancient bricks when he arrived in 1902 to excavate the mound.

The interpretation of biblical prophecy has been discussed at great length by theologians of all types. Dyer argues that a literal fulfillment of the prophecies of Babylon's fall has not occurred; therefore, he *assumes* Babylon will play a significant role in end-time events along with a revived Roman Empire. He therefore views the "Babylon" of Revelation 17 as the "literal rebuilt city of Babylon."[22] From this assumption, Dyer *speculates* that the rise of Saddam Hussein in Iraq and his attempt to rebuild Babylon has prophetic significance.

The "Two Babylons" theory is not new. It has been proposed before, but has not been taken very seriously. Dyer is to be commended for arguing his case carefully and thoroughly, but there are several problems with it.

1. Ancient Babylon has already been destroyed.

Archeological and historical records clearly attest to both the conquest and destruction of ancient Babylon, leaving it in total ruins. General statements, like every stone being discarded, cannot be pressed to literal extremes. Besides, bricks made of clay are not stones. Jesus Himself said of the Temple Mount at Jerusalem, "not one stone here will be left on another; every one will be thrown down" (Matthew 24:2). Yet the "Wailing Wall," comprised of the foundation stones of Herod's Temple Mount, is still standing today. The prophecy was fulfilled when the Romans destroyed Jerusalem in A.D. 70 and tore down the temple. That a few stones remain does not cancel the fulfillment of the prophecy. The structure of the temple came down just as Jesus said it would. To over-literalize prophecy often misses the intent of the prophecy. For example, Malachi predicted that Elijah would come back (Malachi 4:5) and Jesus said that prophecy was fulfilled in John the Baptist (Matthew 11:11-15).

2. Babylon has never returned to her former glory.

The ruins of Babylon are ample testimony to the fulfillment of the prophecies against it. It has been uninhabited for nearly 2,000 years. A few squatters on its fringes do not negate the fact that the greatest city of the ancient world was in fact destroyed as the Hebrew prophets predicted. Saddam Hussein's attempts to refurbish the ancient mound are nothing more than a tourist trap and monument to his own exaggerated opinion of himself. While he may view himself as the modern successor to Hammurabi and Nebuchadnezzar, the rest of the world sees him quite differently. It is highly unlikely that Hussein or anyone else will rebuild ancient Babylon into the "major end-time evil empire," only to have it permanently destroyed again.[23] In fact, God may use the Gulf War to keep Hussein from rebuilding Babylon and protect the prophecy so that Babylon will not be rebuilt. Saddam, like Alexander and Antiochus Epiphanes before him, has seen his hopes shattered.

3. Isaiah and Jeremiah prophesied against ancient Babylon.
Those who believe Iraq will rise to greatness, rebuild Babylon, and finally be destroyed, tend to view Isaiah 13 as a future event when people "come from faraway lands" (Isaiah 13:5), namely, the United States, to destroy Iraq. One could always argue for a dual (or multiple) fulfillment in this passage, but there are several considerations that limit the fulfillment of this prophecy to *ancient* Babylon.

First, Isaiah delivers oracles ("burdens," KJV) against Babylon and ten other of Israel's enemies.[24] Why not take all these oracles as future prophecies yet to be fulfilled? They all speak of total destruction and devastation. The same hermeneutic principles must apply to all or none of these prophecies.

Second, notice that Isaiah predicted that Babylon would be overthrown by the Medes (Isaiah 13:17). This was fulfilled when the alliance of Medes and Persians took the city. To attempt to see the ancient Medes as the Kurds of Iraq, who oppose Hussein, seems a bit stretched and violates the original intention of the prophecy.

4. The "Babylon" of the Book of Revelation is symbolic.
While the Apostle John draws from Old Testament imagery,

he clearly tells us that the Babylon of the future sits on "seven hills" and has ten kings (or kingdoms) within its borders (Revelation 17:9-12). Biblical scholars are virtually unanimous in their agreement that John is talking about Rome, in particular, and an extended European (or revised Roman) political system in the Last Days. This kingdom is so vast that it trades with the kings of the earth, carries on extensive merchandise, is filled with musicians and craftsmen, is arrayed in great wealth, and is "drunk with the blood of the martyrs of Jesus" (Revelation 17:6, KJV).

This prophetic "Babylon" is hardly Iraq! It is, rather, the epitome of a one-world government of Gentile power that will oppose God and the people of God in the Last Days. Rather than being a rebuilt Iraqi Babylon, it is the end-time "Babylon" that is symbolic of all evil, pride, oppression, and power which exalts itself against God.[25] It will combine the best efforts of a collective humanity to rule itself without God. And it will fail!

6

THE NEW WORLD ORDER

It was a far different world when Aldous Huxley wrote *Brave New World* in 1932. Yet the insightful Huxley saw ahead through the labyrinth of the future to a time when the World State would rise to power. In many ways this volume was the most prophetic secular book of the twentieth century.

Instead of the Big Brother of George Orwell's *1984*, Huxley foresaw a world gone mad on materialism and pleasure seeking to deaden its conscience against the value-emptied culture of high technology. His vision of human fertilization "farms" seemed absolutely unthinkable. Artificial insemination and genetic selection sounded like something out of a science fiction horror movie, but somehow Huxley knew the seeds of the future had already been sown in the past.

Huxley pictured the future as the mindless pursuit of one's existence, controlled by machines and soothed by the endless pursuit of pleasure. The past would become meaningless and intellectual, and noble pursuits would give way to the all-consuming pursuit of pleasure. One of the most intriguing dialogues in his book takes place between Fanny and Lenina, the one small-talking about the changes in society and the other small-talking about clothes, belts, shoes, and jewelry. The world of the future which Huxley foresaw was one that would readily sacrifice its principles for pleasure. It was a new world, unified politically and economically, whose god was itself—the World State.

NEW WINDS ARE BLOWING ACROSS EUROPE

President Bush has talked frequently about the "New Europe" and the "New World Order." In a live CNN broadcast on February 6, 1991, the President talked about the coming prosperity and stability of the "New Europe" in his address to the Economic Club of New York City. He seems upbeat and hopeful when addressing this subject. There is a gleam in his eye as though he is touching something bigger than life.

The world is changing with breathtaking speed. Old ways of doing business and old styles of leadership are rapidly disappearing. Old ideas and beliefs are swept away in an instant of macro-change. *Megatrends* John Naisbitt calls them.[1]

Naisbitt predicts a global economic boom for the 1990s. His projections are based on growing telecommunications and free trade among all nations. The United States, Europe, and Japan are the potential winners in the global bonanza. Even the global lifestyle will increase dramatically with extensive international travel, trade, and technology advances.

Prior to the Gulf War, the 1990s were being hailed as the

most exciting and encouraging times in recent human history. "Never before has the prospect of world peace and prosperity seemed so promising," wrote one author prior to the invasion of Kuwait.[2] How quickly things changed when the Desert Shield was thrown up and then attacked as the Desert Storm!

THE PARTY'S OVER— THE COMMUNIST PARTY!

Nineteen eighty-nine was the year of transformation in Eastern Europe. The walls of communism came crashing down so quickly that even the most ardent anti-communists were shocked. The astonished world watched, stunned with near disbelief as the Iron Curtain was torn down. More than forty years had passed since Winston Churchill's famous speech at Westminster College in 1946, when he said, "An Iron Curtain has fallen across the Continent."

The Iron Curtain mentality and that of the Cold War was a harsh reality we all lived with in those years following World War II. It took the joy out of the Allied victory over Hitler's Germany because it left a divided world behind. Eastern Europe was dragged into a Soviet empire. In many ways the wars that followed in Korea and Vietnam were but ugly cancers left behind by the failure to resolve the spoils of victory from World War II.

Then came the unexpected! Mikhail Gorbachev made it clear that the Soviet Union would no longer interfere in the internal policies of the Warsaw Pact nations of Eastern Europe. For nearly a decade, people had been crying for democracy and freedom. The Solidarity movement had shaken Poland to the core. Though often criticized, Billy Graham preached in one communist country after another. He forged ahead believing God could make a difference behind the Iron Curtain—and He did. The evangelical revival in Romania exploded after Billy Graham's visit, and within weeks the communist dictatorship was overthrown.

Eastern bloc countries began to open to others too whose messages of life and hope in Christ brought a new wave of demand for religious freedom. Rev. Vernon Brewer, vice president of Liberty University in Virginia, took hundreds of students behind the Iron Curtain in the 1980s to expose them to the future potential of evangelistic enterprise in Eastern Europe. Today the doors are wide open to Bibles, commentaries, missionaries, theological educators, and Christian workers.

EAST MEETS WEST

When Bush and Gorbachev met at Malta, off the coast of Italy, *Time* magazine (December 11, 1989) flashed their smiling faces on the cover with the startling headline: BUILDING A NEW WORLD. Change was under way that would not be denied. In Gorbachev's meeting with Pope John Paul II, he said, "Having embarked upon the road of radical reform, the socialist countries are crossing the line beyond which there is no return to the past."[3]

While some fear this is all a ploy to soften up the West, neutralize the United States, and undermine the NATO military alliance, it is clear that the cat is out of the bag! It is highly unlikely that the Soviets could regain control over their former satellite nations without long and serious military action against them.

The real question now facing the Russian Soviets is whether they can even hold onto their own fifteen republics! Independence movements are aflame everywhere within the

Soviet Union—in Latvia, Estonia, Lithuania, Moldavia, and the six Muslim republics along the southern border. Dave Hunt observes, "One thing is certain: Much of Lenin's evil empire has gone up in flames, and the unlikely arsonist . . . was the Soviet president himself."[4]

A NEW WORLD ORDER?

The prospect of democracy, followed by capitalism, is sweeping across Eastern Europe, but it cannot survive without great difficulties. The emerging independence movement will likely fuel rising nationalism and could lead to the kind of conflicts that often were going on in Europe prior to World War I. Ethnic enemies within Yugoslavia threaten to split the country apart.

Despite these challenges, the prospects for peace and economic cooperation are bright, but they may only be realized under some kind of strong personal leadership. George Bush sees himself in that kind of role. *Time* recently reported that Bush had resolved to "shape the new world order emerging in the aftermath of the cold war."[5] At the same time, it is obvious that Gorbachev sees himself in that role as well.

Public policy makers are now assuming that the new order will only work if the United States and the Soviet Union resolve to work together through the United Nations to provide a collective security for the future world. This theme certainly came through loud and clear in President Bush's televised address at the start of the offensive against Iraq. Twice in that speech he referred to the prospects of an internationally cooperative "new world order." Bush said, "We have before us the opportunity to forge for ourselves and for future generations a *new world order.* . . . When we are successful, and we will be, we have a real chance at this *new world order,* an order in which a credible UN can use its peace-keeping role to fulfill the promise and vision of the UN's founders."[6]

A NEW REFORMATION?

In a powerful and insightful editorial in *Newsweek,* George Will compared the startling changes that are taking place in Europe to the Reformation of the sixteenth century.

> It is just 60 miles from Berlin to Wittenberg, where the 34-year-old Luther nailed his 95 theses to the church door. Four years later at the Diet of Worms he spoke [the] words that define the modern frame of mind . . . "Here I stand, I can do no other." The primary idea of the Reformation was the primacy of individual conscience. It has been the high-octane fuel of all subsequent history.[7]

In Will's assessment, the greatest failure of communism was its ideological assault on individualism. Socialism had impoverished every facet of individual life. People had simply had "enough" and said so! Their spontaneous grass-roots revolt was like a gale-force wind hurling across Eastern Europe, knocking down every obstacle to democracy.

Europe is changing rapidly. Ideological barriers are falling everywhere, borders are blurring, and the continent is coming together. The new "chunnel" (tunnel) under the English Channel, completed in 1990, will make it possible to drive from Paris to London in a few hours. For the first time in history, England is land-connected to the rest of Europe! Not only governments and politics, but even the geographics of Europe are changing.

IT ALL POINTS TO 1992

"Europoria" is the mood of exuberance is sweeping Europe these days. Spain will host both the Summer Olympics and the World's Fair in 1992, but the real excitement is the economic integration of Western Europe coming in 1992. The old dream of European unity will become a reality by December 31, 1992, when the twelve members of the European Economic Community (EEC) will unite their economic markets to create the largest trading bloc and free market economy in the world.

Time magazine recently declared, "Project 1992 has given fresh momentum . . . to taking Western Europe further down the road to unity."[8] Now, with the collapse of communism in Eastern Europe, the prospect for a United Europe may finally become a reality in the not too distant future. While several leaders are involved in the "Continental Express," France's Jacques Delors has been the chief engineer since becoming President of the European Commission in 1985. He was personally responsible for setting 1992 as the target date to make it all happen. Delors has called for a unified currency for all of Europe, common European passports, and even the possibility of political unification—all in the name of material prosperity and success. "We must build Europe every day," he has said. "We must go all the way."[9] His tenacity drove Margaret Thatcher out of office and even forced French Socialist Francois Mitterrand to get in step with the project.

It is no wonder Delors has earned the nickname, "Mr. Europe." *U.S. News & World Report* predicts a unified Western Europe by 1995, adding, "Less passionate crusaders than Jacques Delors are squinting at the year 2000—and holding their breath."[10] Whatever the pace or the obstacles ahead, the idea is alive and well. Britain's new Prime Minister, John

Major, is one of its strongest advocates. In December 1990 the European Commission approved major steps to propel the EEC beyond the unified economic market already scheduled for 1992 toward real political union in the future. The goal is for the European Economic Community (EEC) to become the European Community (EC). A light-blue flag with a circle of twelve stars has already been prepared.

WHY ALL THE EXCITEMENT?

Megatrends 2000 addresses the question of what 1992 is all about with a concise and practical list:[11]

- 1992 means that a Greek lawyer will be able to set up a practice in Copenhagen and that a Spanish shoe company could open a shop unhindered in Dublin.
- 1992 means that a Japanese or American businessman can fly into one European Community country, pass through customs once, and then visit the other eleven without seeing another customs or immigration official.
- 1992 means that a Portuguese bank can be the partner of a new venture in the Paris fashion industry.
- 1992 means goods and people moving as easily from France to Germany as they can from California to Oregon.
- 1992 means that there will be more competition at all levels of the single market, bringing greater choice of attractively priced goods and services.

HOW WILL IT WORK?

The philosophy behind the dream is fairly simple—forge Europe into one cohesive market in order to compete with the

United States and Japan on a global scale. In order for this to happen, three things must occur and all the rest will fall in place.

First, *physical* barriers, such as customs posts, frontier controls, and product restrictions, will be removed. This will eliminate long lines and mountains of paperwork at the borders of each member country.

Second, *technical* barriers involving different standards and regulations to which businesses have to comply will be unified. Any goods or services lawfully produced in one member country can be marketed in another automatically.

Third, *fiscal* barriers, such as luxury taxes, food, wine, and hotel taxes which vary greatly from one country to another, will be standardized. The result will bring "a dramatic change in the world of European retailing," states Eric Salama of the Henley Centre for Forecasting in London.[12] This will also improve the ability of retailers to obtain products from all the member countries of the European Economic Community.

However, Salama warns, the consumer tastes vary enormously across Europe and not all goods will sell as well in every member nation. Old habits, culture, and language barriers will still remain. However, the big goal of unifying the internal market, proposed when the Treaty of Rome was signed in 1957, will now be fully realized in 1992.

The original treaty envisioned *both* an economic and political unification of Europe before the end of the twentieth century. The passing of the Single European Act, by the members of the EEC, now makes that dream a potential reality in the near future. Nicholas Colchester states, "The agreement to lift national controls on the flow of capital is, in my view, the most striking concession to the idea of a single market so far made."[13]

POWER OF THE COMPUTER

The real key to making the New Europe work will be the personal computer. "Computer power," writes John Lamb, editor of *Computer Weekly,* "is now at the executive's fingertips ... linking computers, large and small, to a central clearing house."[14] The computer spreadsheet will replace the pocket calculator as financial transactions in the New Europe leap across computer screens from businesses to banks to manufacturers to retailers and even into private homes all across the continent.

The high-speed computer network across Europe will bring the continent together economically and eventually politically in a way that no military action ever could. The political integration of Europe will ride on the shoulders of computer integration.

The impersonal computer screen will carry visual images, by means of scanners which "turn pictures into a digital form suitable for processing and able to be displayed on a computer screen."[15]

All of this information will be stored and processed in a gigantic computer at the EEC's central headquarters in Brussels, Belgium. The monstrous computer actually has been dubbed the "Beast." Eventually it will be used to control all of Europe's economic transactions.

HAVEN'T WE READ THIS SOMEWHERE BEFORE?

While European businesses are awash with excitement about the prospects of 1992, many evangelicals are more than a bit concerned. "This sounds like Bible prophecy," a friend remarked recently. "Doesn't the Bible talk about a one-world government, economic controls, and the "image of the Beast" as having something to do with the Antichrist?"

The Book of Revelation does make some startling predictions about life on this planet in the Last Days. It tells us of a powerful leader who will arise promising peace and prosperity, only to deceive the world into worshiping him. Theologians debate whether he is a person or an evil system. In either case, his/its ability to control humanity in the last times will have much to do with his control of the economy. The Apocalypse predicts, "No one could buy or sell unless he had the mark, which is the name of the Beast or the number of his name" (Revelation 13:17). The Scripture also warns against the "image" of the Beast that could talk and deceive the inhabitants of earth into worshiping him/it.

Needless to say, evangelicals are concerned about where all this might lead. There is certainly nothing wrong with computers and electronic imagery and cashless financial transactions. The big problem is that it all becomes one more giant step for impersonal technology. We are already prisoners of our own technology and will likely become more enslaved by it. Electric windows in an automobile are great until they won't work on a hot day and you are left sweltering in a closed-up automobile. Technology itself is neither moral nor immoral. The ultimate issue is *how* we use that technology or how *it* uses us.

MODERN TOWER OF BABEL?

The official poster of the Council of Europe depicts the European Community as the Tower of Babel under construction, with twelve stars representing the twelve nations of the New Europe. The hope of the future is captured in the caption: "Europe: Many Tongues, One Voice."

An evangelical writer has also noticed that the European Edition of the *Wall Street Journal,* for the second quarter of 1990, contained an insert from IBM that also depicted the New Europe as the Tower of Babel.[16] This may all be mere coincidence, but it makes one wonder —Bible prophecy predicts the rise of a symbolic "Babylon" that will control the economic and political world of the Last Days. Is this beginning to happen before our very eyes?

BYZANTIUM REVISITED

Daniel's prophecy of the last empire, with two legs and ten toes (Daniel 2), generally has been interpreted as Byzantine Rome (east and west) and an eventual revived "Rome" (or Europe) of the Last Days. The two legs symbolize the two divisions of the Roman Empire since Constantine moved the capital to Byzantium (Constantinople).

The eastern part of the Roman Empire reached from Constantinople northward into the fringes of Russia, eastward through the Middle East, and south toward Egypt and North Africa. The essential language in the Eastern Empire was Greek, and the predominant religion was the Eastern Orthodox Church. Their missionary enterprise took Christianity to Russia and the Ukraine in the tenth and eleventh centuries. For this reason the Russian Orthodox Church and the Russian language, which is written in a Greek-influenced alphabet, owe much to the eastern wing of the old Roman Empire.

The western part of the Roman Empire covered most of Continental Europe and extended all the way to Great Britain. In the West, Latin was the predominant language and the Roman Catholic Church was the predominant religion. British Christianity and, in turn, American Christianity were influenced more by this wing of the empire. For example, American churches usually follow the Catholic dates for Christmas and Easter, as opposed to the Orthodox dates.

Many believe that the New Europe of the future may well be an economically and politically United Europe encompassing much of the old Roman Empire. The Rome Treaty itself even suggests Rome as a possible capital for a unified government. This does not mean that the common market of 1992 is necessarily all bad or that Christians ought to throw away their computers or that electronic bar codes are the "mark of the beast." But the world could be marching in concert to a drummer it doesn't even know is there—Satan.

HERE COMES THE BEAST

The Bible depicts the Antichrist as the "Beast coming out of the sea" whose "fatal wound had been healed" (Revelation 13:1-11). This term has been variously applied—to the assassination of some great leader who rises in Europe in the Last Days or to the recovery of the corpse of the old Roman Empire aided by false religion, "the false prophet."

The interpretation of these figures hinges on whether they are individuals or collective entities or both. The casting of the Beast and false prophet into the lake of fire (Revelation 19:20-21) sounds personal, as though they are two individuals. But the symbolism of the seven hills and ten horns sounds like a political system. Perhaps it is best to see them as both a leader and a system which he controls.

The Apostle John said that the spirit of false teaching, already active in the first century, was a form of the spirit of Antichrist. He wrote: "This is the spirit of the antichrist, which you have heard is coming and even now is already in the world" (1 John 4:3). In the broadest sense, the Antichrist is already here. The Revelation tells us that Satan is the real power behind him, and Satan has been around for a very long time.

It would seem to me that we must reconcile all of these aspects of prophecy by recognizing: (1) that the spirit of Antichrist (Satan) is already operating in the world; (2) there will come a political, material, economic, and religious world system in the Last Days which is in itself "antichrist"; (3) there will finally emerge a powerful individual who will control that system and use it for evil against God's people.

By allowing the full fruition of these prophecies to touch every possible aspect of this future evil enterprise, we can let the *facts* of prophecy stand clear from our own limiting *assumptions* and *speculations*.

A MATTER OF TIMING

The ultimate problem regarding prophecies of the end times is determining what time it is right now. It has been a common error throughout church history for Christians to *assume* they were living in the Last Days. Once that time frame is accepted, one can speculate that any contemporary event may be a fulfillment of prophecy. But if our timing is off, the entire *speculation* will collapse.

The global trends emerging today point to the *possibility* of changes necessary for the events of prophecy to unfold. But this does not prove they will develop in that manner. For example, the grand experiment of the European Community could fail disastrously and come to naught. The Soviet Union may or may not continue toward democracy. It may or may not move closer to the New Europe. There is no way to know these things without speculating.

Christ may return today or He may not come for 200

years, but some things are certain because the *facts* of prophecy say so:

- Wars, conflicts, and natural disasters will continue throughout the present age (Matthew 24–26).
- The Gospel must continue to be preached until Christ returns (Matthew 24:14).
- False prophets will deceive many throughout the present age (Matthew 24:24).
- No one knows the date of Christ's return (Matthew 24:36).
- Believers are to remain faithful in their service to Christ and be ready for Him to come at any time (Matthew 24:42-51).
- "Terrible times" will come in the Last Days, signified by a rebellious and indulgent society (2 Timothy 3:1-5).
- A great deceiver will arise in the Last Days and lead the world astray (2 Thessalonians 2:1-12).
- The church will be "caught up" in the Rapture when Christ comes for His own (1 Thessalonians 4:13-18).
- A time of Great Tribulation will burst upon the world as a result of God's judgment against sin (Revelation 6–19).
- Jesus Christ will come at the end of the Tribulation at the Battle of Armageddon to overthrow the unholy trinity: Satan, Antichrist, and false prophet (Revelation 19:11-21).
- Christ shall rule on earth for a thousand years in His millennial reign (Revelation 20:1-6).
- Satan, death, and hell will all be cast into the lake of fire after the Millennium and the new heavens and new earth will usher in the eternal kingdom (Revelation 21–22).

This is the coming new world order which shall last forever. It is not the device or plan of men; it is the eternal kingdom of God, which reigns over all the universe from eternity to eternity. To which we say, "Come quickly, Lord Jesus!"

7

CAN THERE BE LASTING PEACE IN THE MIDDLE EAST?

"Get rid of that woman!" she shouted, pointing to the door.

"But this was all your idea," her husband pleaded, torn between his two wives and their sons.

"Get rid of that slave woman and her son," Sarah insisted, "for that slave woman's son will never share in the inheritance with my son, Isaac."

They had waited so long to have children—what a tragedy to be feuding over them now! Abraham and Sarah had left the city of Ur, not far from modern Kuwait. They were wealthy and prosperous, but their hearts were empty without an heir to their fortune.

As the years rolled by, they considered adoption, but God promised Abraham a son of his own (Genesis 15:1-7). But as Sarah grew older, she knew she was beyond childbearing age. Finally, in desperation, she suggested that Abraham have a child by her Egyptian slave girl, Hagar. But when Hagar conceived a baby, tension arose between her and Sarah.

WHAT COULD GO WRONG?

In essence, Abraham had taken the attitude: What could go wrong? Plenty! And it has been going wrong between the descendants of Abraham ever since. The Bible tells us they had been in Canaan (modern Israel) for ten years when Hagar conceived Ishmael. At one point, Hagar even tried to run away, but God intervened and sent her back with the promise that He would increase her descendants through Ishmael.

Then God made a strange prediction (Genesis 16:11-12). He told Hagar she would have a son and that she should name him Ishmael ("God hears"). But then God warned her that he would be a "wild donkey," whose hand would be against every man and every man's hand would be against him. "He will live in hostility toward all his brothers," God explained. Nevertheless, God promised to bless him and to make of him a "great nation" (Genesis 21:18). Over the centuries of time, Ishmael's descendants came to be known as the Arabs.

In the meantime, Sarah's son, Isaac, became the forefather of the Jews. Isaac's son Jacob received the promise of the messianic line. Later in life, his name was changed to Israel ("prince of God") and his twelve sons became the forefathers of the twelve tribes of Israel.

A DIVIDED FAMILY

In a moment of weakness, perhaps even desperation, Abraham put reason above revelation and then lived to suffer the consequences. God had promised him a son and meant to bring that son into the world by his legal wife, Sarah. But assuming herself to be too old to have a child, Sarah thought God must have meant for *him* to have a child, but not by her.

Once Sarah read "between the lines" of God's revelation,

she rationalized that He must have meant something other than what He had said. At any rate, because of this decision Abraham's family would be divided forever.

We can hardly blame Hagar for what happened. She was a slave girl; she was their personal property. Hagar had no rights of her own. She was expected to cooperate with whatever she was told. Once she got pregnant, however, she seemed to gloat in it all and Sarah felt despised by her. That haughty attitude set the stage for what followed.

The Bible tells us that Abraham was eighty-six years old when Ishmael was born (Genesis 16:16). But then there followed thirteen silent years in the sacred record. The very next verse (Genesis 17:1) states that Abraham was ninety-nine years old when God spoke and confirmed His covenant with Abraham. Was there no new message from God in all that time? Was He displeased with Abraham? Had He paused to grieve over the pain that would come in the years to follow? We are not told. There is no explanation given.

A COVENANT WITH ISRAEL

When God finally broke His thirteen-year silence, He told Abraham that He would bless Ishmael, but He would make His covenant with Isaac (Genesis 17:18-21). When Sarah received this news, she laughed because she had passed menopause ("the manner of women," [Genesis 18:11, KJV]). But God miraculously intervened to give her conception by her husband, and a miracle-birth child came into the world.

The Bible does not say that Isaac was a better person than Ishmael. They both had their shortcomings. But the Bible emphasizes the sovereign purpose of God in the covenant He made with Abraham and confirmed to Isaac and reconfirmed to Jacob (Israel).[1] It was an eternal covenant, sealed in blood.

It was God's promise to bring a Redeemer into the world through the nation of Israel.

Jesus Christ was the promised Redeemer. He was the Son of the Covenant, born of the seed of Israel, the descendant of Abraham (Matthew 1:1-2). He was God incarnate in human flesh as the ultimate fulfillment of God's covenant promises to Abraham. He is the One who died for our sins and made salvation available to all people: men, women, Jews, Arabs, Gentiles, bond, free, black, and white.

God's salvation is not limited to any one people. He is the God who created us all and who commands all people to repent (Acts 17:30). He set apart the people of Israel to receive His glory, His Covenant, His Law, and His promises, and He used them to protect the human ancestry of Christ (Romans 9:4-5).

ONLY A REMNANT

Despite Israel's advantages, the Apostle Paul said, "Only the remnant will be saved" (Romans 9:27) during the Church Age, until the "full number of the Gentiles has come in" (Romans 11:25). In other words, the majority of converts to Christ during the present era will be Gentiles.

This raises the question of the eternality and current validity of the covenant with Israel. Paul himself, an Israelite, asked, "Did God reject His people?" Then he answered emphatically, "By no means!" (Romans 11:1) Paul explained that "at the present time there is a remnant chosen by grace" (Romans 11:5). These are Israelites who have come to faith in Jesus as their Messiah.

During the Church Age, all people, including Jews and Arabs, are called to faith in Jesus Christ, the Prince of Peace. Only in Him can there be lasting peace between mortal enemies. In Christ, all men are equal brothers. There is neither Jew nor Arab nor Gentile. We are one in Christ.

This great truth bonds the hearts of all Christians, no matter what their national or ethnic origin. No one group is better than another. No one person takes precedence over another. All are equal in Christ. It was this truth—that a slave and a master were equal brothers in Christ—that broke the bond of slavery in the Roman world. When we kneel before Christ and submit to His lordship, we find the ground is level at the cross.

IRRECONCILABLE DIFFERENCES?

The great tragedy of the ongoing crisis in the Middle East is that without Christ there is no hope of lasting peace. Men may talk of peace, plan for peace, and work for peace, but there will be no peace. The irreconcilable differences between the Arabs and the Jews go back 4,000 years. These old hatreds and prejudices do not go away by human efforts. No amount of education, psychology, social welfare, or government planning can eradicate that unresolvable hatred. It can only be corrected by the love of Christ.

This leaves the Christian in a precarious position. On the one hand, he is to preach the Gospel to all people, including Arabs and Jews. He is to love them both with the love of Christ. We must be careful to communicate that truth to both groups. On the other hand, most Christians believe that God is not finished with His people Israel. He still has a plan for their future after the "times of the Gentiles" have been fulfilled. Therefore, we sympathize with Israel's right to exist as a people and a nation.

This tension calls us as the servants of Christ to love two peoples who do not love each other. We must demonstrate the power of the Gospel to both groups. It will not be easy to affirm Israel's right to her land without offending Arabs. Also, it will not be easy to express our concern for the Palestinians without offending the Israelis, but we must—for Christ's sake and the Gospel.

Christians must also guard against the temptation to hate Arabs, or any Muslims, because of the war in the Middle East. We can rightly affirm the just cause of war as a response to injustice, without hating our enemies. This is never easy to do, especially when you have lost a loved one to that enemy. Despite the war with Iraq, we must pray that God will give us grace not to hate the Iraqis, but to demonstrate the love of Christ to them.

INEVITABLE DESTINY?

One of the tragedies of the war will be a widening division between some of the Arabs and the West. On the one hand, we have demonstrated the possibility of cooperation as Western and Saudi flags have flown side by side. But on the other hand, there is a deep resentment toward the United States in the hearts of many Arab peoples.

Many have speculated that the current crisis has set the prophetic stage for the future.[2] On the one hand, the world is calling for a peaceful resolution of the conflict. This will require greater cooperation between the Arabs and the West. But on the other hand, the old hatreds remain deeper than ever. The barbaric cries of "Death" to all who oppose them do not give much hope to a lasting, peaceful Arab solution.

This is the great dilemma that has confronted the Jews for centuries. They have often tried to live at peace with their Muslim neighbors.[3] History attests to the fact that Jewish communities often flourished among the Arabs—in Egypt,

Syria, Iraq, and Iran. But sooner or later, the Jews came under persecution and often fled for their lives.

This leaves the question of future Arab-Israeli relations very much in doubt. The Jews were without a national home for nearly 2,000 years after the Romans destroyed Jerusalem in A.D. 70. For centuries they were forced to live among Christians and Arabs alike as they wandered the earth in search of a home. Finally, in 1897 an Austrian Jew named Theodore Hertzl cried out to the leaders of Europe. "There is a land without a people," he said, "and there is a people without a land. Give the land without a people to the people without a land."[4] Hertzl wrote the book *Judenstat*, calling for the rebirth of the State of Israel. At the same time, he convened the World Zionist Congress in Switzerland to discuss his hopes and plans for the future.

In the meantime, British General Allenby took Jerusalem from the Turks without firing a shot on December 9, 1917. The Turks had allied with the Germans during World War I and their losses included Palestine. The British passed the Balfour Declaration calling for the establishment of an independent Jewish state in Palestine. On May 24, 1920, the League of Nations ratified Britain's mandate over Palestine and opened the door for Jews to return to their ancient homeland.

PROPHETIC FULFILLMENT

Many evangelicals believe that the Jews' return to Palestine is the most significant evidence of fulfilled prophecy in our time. John Phillips says, "It is one of the greatest signs of the end times."[5] He points to Isaiah 60:9-10 as dramatic testimony to this prophetic fulfillment: "Surely the isles shall wait for me, and the ships of Tarshish [Europe] first, to bring thy sons from far. . . . And the sons of strangers shall build up thy walls, and their kings shall minister unto thee" (KJV).

When the United Nations met to vote on the partitioning of Palestine on November 27, 1947, there was little hope of Israel getting the necessary two-thirds vote. At the last minute, the Soviet Union surprised everyone and voted *for* the establishment of the State of Israel and the vote passed! On May 14, 1948 the British High Commissioner for Palestine stepped down and the Zionist Council in Tel Aviv proclaimed the State of Israel established with David Ben Gurion as Prime Minister and Chaim Weizmann as President.

Several Arab states, including Egypt, Jordan, and Iraq, immediately proclaimed a holy war against the newly reborn Israel and attacked on all sides. But to the world's great surprise, Israel not only defended itself but forced the Arabs to accept a truce. In 1956 Nasser of Egypt tried to attack Israel and was decisively turned back. Again, in 1967, Nasser provoked the Israelis into the Six-Day War. By the time it was over, Israel had conquered the Sinai, the old city of Jerusalem, the West Bank of the Jordan, and the Golan Heights. Israel's military superiority shocked the secular world. But biblical scholars began to take seriously the prophets' predictions that the Jews would "never again . . . be uprooted from the land I have given them" (Amos 9:15).

By 1973 Anwar Sadat was in power as Egypt's President. His independence became clear when he threw the Russian military advisers out of the country. But increased tension over the oil embargo lingered. Sadat caught the world by surprise when he attacked the Sinai Peninsula while Syria attacked the Golan Heights on October 6, 1973—Yom Kippur, the Jewish Day of Atonement. Again, the Israelis won a decisive victory, but this time with heavy losses.

In the years that followed, Sadat made an incredible statesmanlike move and traveled to Israel to meet with Prime

Minister Menachem Begin and to address the Knesset, the Israeli congress at Jerusalem. Later, Begin and Sadat met with American President Jimmy Carter in 1978 at Camp David, Maryland to discuss the Camp David Peace Accords. Their goal was to establish a lasting peace in the Middle East. In March of 1979 Israel and Egypt signed a formal peace treaty in Washington, D.C. A leading Arab nation had committed itself to peace with Israel!

ESCALATING ESCHATOLOGICAL DRAMA

In the meantime, major changes were under way throughout the Middle East. Muammar Qaddafi took over Libya, nationalized its oil industry, and began threatening international terrorism. The United States responded with brief, but effective military action. In 1979 an Islamic revolution in Iran overthrew the Shah and brought the Ayatollah Khomeini to power in a newly established Islamic republic. About the same time, Saddam Hussein came to power in Iraq and launched a war with Iran from 1980 to 1988, over territorial disputes. A cease-fire came in August of 1988. But two years later, in August of 1990, Hussein invaded Kuwait and brought the wrath of the United Nations down on Iraq.

In many ways, Israel's survival in the midst of an Arab sea of humanity is indeed miraculous! While one could speculate that their presence in the Holy Land may be only temporary and may not be their final return, this seems unlikely. They seem to be there to stay. Many, including Dr. John Walvoord, chancellor of Dallas Theological Seminary, believe the times of the Gentiles may be coming to a close and the great end-times drama is about to unfold.[6]

Many evangelicals point to God's promise to Abraham that God would bless them that blessed him and curse those who cursed him (Genesis 12:3) as binding on nations and how they treat Israel. The Prophet Jeremiah put it even more strikingly when he said: "But all who devour you [Israel] will be devoured; all your enemies will go into exile. Those who plunder you will be plundered; all who make spoil of you I will despoil" (Jeremiah 30:16).

Whatever one's view of eschatology, he must admit that Israel has suffered unreasonably at the hand of her neighbors. To be sure, the Arabs have genuine concerns of their own, but such unreasonable acts as Iraq's unprovoked missile attacks against Israel certainly do not make sympathizers out of most Americans or Europeans. Nor do such acts of terrorism commend the Islamic faith to the rest of the watching world.

PROMISES OF PEACE

There is something shocking and horrifying about war that makes us all shudder. The highway to death, its ultimate finality makes it terrifying. Therefore, in the midst of every war, the cries for peace begin to surface. One would think that educated modern people would avoid the destructiveness of war at all costs. But there is something basically destructive in the psyche of human depravity that makes war an inevitable reality.

Despite the continual reoccurrence of war, peace efforts are constantly being made to stop conflicts and propose settlements for opposing parties. This has been an especially difficult prospect in the Middle East, where underlying tensions go back for centuries and where religious issues provoke bitterness, hatred, and even war. This is why a proposed peace settlement in the Middle East raises such high hopes. It promises an end to hostilities and the beginning of a new order for the future.

The immediate solution would seem to be a peace treaty "that settles disputes, disarms antagonists, and provides absolute guarantees," writes Walvoord.[7] Such a treaty would probably be backed up by military force, but whatever settlement is reached will only be temporary in nature. Conflicts are bound to resurge again and again.

THREATS OF WAR

The Bible predicts two things in Israel's future: *peace* and *war*. The Old Testament Scriptures indicate that a great world leader will come onto the scene promising lasting peace in the Middle East and signing a peace treaty with Israel. Most evangelicals believe this leader will arise from the European Community, though some think he may be from the Middle East itself.

We can only *speculate* at this point as to *how* that peace settlement may come about in the near future. The continued threat of war, an economic crisis, or an oil shortage could all be factors in triggering further conflict in the Middle East. Whatever the cause, the call for peace will out cry the call for war. The Bible predicts a treaty (covenant) between Israel and a powerful world leader will result in peace and prosperity for the nation and people of Israel (Daniel 9:27ff.).

But this peace will be short-lived—only three and one-half years. For in the middle of Daniel's prophetic seventieth week, the world leader will break his covenant with Israel. Many evangelicals believe this will happen at the midpoint of the seven-year Tribulation Period. Once he has deceived Israel, he will turn against them in a violent persecution for another three and one-half years. Jesus called this time the "Great Tribulation" (Matthew 24:21, KJV). Jeremiah called it "the time of Jacob's Trouble" (Jeremiah 30:7). The prophetic Scriptures indicate that God will use the Great Tribulation to awaken Israel to the truth about their Messiah.

In Israel's most desperate hour, the Lord Jesus, the Prince of Peace, will return to spare Israel and bring His resurrected bride, the church, back with Him to rule in His millennial kingdom on earth. Jesus Himself warned: "If those days had not been cut short, no one would survive" (Matthew 24:22). But God, in His great wisdom and mercy, has promised to spare the world for a better future when there shall be peace for a thousand years while our Lord reigns in Jerusalem upon the throne of David.

SETTING THE STAGE
FOR THE END

The prophets of Israel predicted that the Jews would eventually return to the Promised Land and that Israel would be reestablished as a nation before the end of the "times of the Gentiles." Jesus predicted, "Jerusalem will be trampled on by the Gentiles until the times of the Gentiles are fulfilled" (Luke 21:24). It would seem that time is running out for the Gentiles and that the stage is now set for the end times.

It is always possible that the end is hundreds of years into the future, but it is not very probable. The precarious nature of international events and the ever-present threat of nuclear war remind all of us how near the end could actually be.

It is also possible that Israel's present return to the Holy Land will end in failure and they will be expelled, only to return again later in fulfillment of prophecy. But again, this is not very probable. It would seem that God has set the stage for the end just as the Bible predicted. It seems unlikely He would not choose to use this setting to bring about the end that Jesus and the prophets predicted.

The exact timing of end-times events may be indefinite, but several prophetic elements are now in place:

- Israel is back in the Promised Land for the first time in nearly 2,000 years.
- The Arab nations seem bent on driving Israel into the Mediterranean Sea.
- The intervention of the major Western powers in the Middle East indicates the "times of the Gentiles" are still operable.
- Attempted peace settlements, though desirable, seem destined to failure in resolving the Arab-Israeli conflict.
- Popular resentment against Israel among the Arab peoples is deeper than ever since the Gulf War.
- Iraq's attempt to rally the Arabs into a *jihad* ("holy war") against Israel shows how quickly an Arab coalition could form and invade Israel in the end times.
- The economic and political unification of Europe seems more likely than at any other time in recent history, possibly fulfilling Daniel's prophecies of a great end-times "revived" Roman Empire.
- The stage is now set for a prominent world leader to arise from the West, promising to bring peace to the world.
- A global economy is now upon us. It is only a matter of time until the whole world is one economic unit, waiting to be taken over by a sinister power.
- The potential of nuclear war remains an ever-present reality in the world's march to Armageddon.

While we must be careful not to set dates or to speculate irresponsibly, we certainly can discern that time is running out for our world. Man's clever ingenuity has bailed him out of disaster on numerous occasions during the Cold War years of the late twentieth century. But humankind may be running out of options. It may all be over sooner than we think.

8

PROPHECIES OF
THE END TIMES

Many people believe we are living in the "end times," when
the world will be plunged into a series of cataclysmic wars.
By the time these wars end, perhaps as much as three-fourths
of the earth's population will be destroyed. "Armageddon
theology" is the popular designation for biblical prophecies
about the end of the world.

In the secular mind such beliefs are little understood.
Some have even gone so far as to accuse evangelicals of trying to hasten the end by advocating "a nuclear war as a divine
instrument to punish the wicked and complete God's plan
for history."[1] Many seem to think that because evangelicals
look forward to the second coming of Christ, they will try to
hasten that event, hoping to escape suffering the consequences of Armageddon themselves.

No right-thinking person wants war, no matter what his
views of the end times. We all sense the ominous finality of
the predictions about the end and pray that God will stay His
hand of judgment. But only a fool could think that humans
are clever enough to avoid a final confrontation of disastrous

consequences. We may dodge the apocalyptic bullet a few more times, but sooner or later, we will have to face the final moment of history.

DEFINING OUR TERMS

Eschatology is the general theological term for the study of the end times. It comes from the New Testament Greek word *eschatos*, meaning last or latter. Thus, biblical history moves from a starting point with Creation (Genesis 1:1) and progresses toward a final consummation of all things. The Bible itself describes it like this: "Then the end will come, when He [Christ] hands over the kingdom to God the Father after He has destroyed all dominion, authority and power" (1 Corinthians 15:24).

Several biblical words describe eschatological events.[2]

Last Days. "Last" and "latter" are adjectives that describe the times just before the end of the age. Paul said, "There will be terrible times in the Last Days" (2 Timothy 3:1), and "In the latter times some shall depart from the faith" (1 Timothy 4:1, KJV). Peter said, "In the last days scoffers will come" who deny the promise of Christ's return (2 Peter 3:3).

End of the Age. The "end" (Greek, *telos*) points to the final outcome of all things. Jesus had this in mind when He said, "But the end is not yet" (Matthew 24:6, KJV) and "then the end will come" (Matthew 24:14). "Age" (Greek, *aion*) is generally translated "world" in the *King James Version*, as in Matthew 24:3, "the end of the world." Unfortunately, most think of this as the end of the earth, whereas the Greek phrase only means, "the end of the age" (NIV). This points to a time when the present age will conclude, but it will not be the end of the planet.

Consummation of the Age. This term (Greek, *sunteleia*) is similar to "end of the age" and expresses the final unfolding of all things. Jesus promises to be with us "to the very end of the age" (Matthew 28:20).

Second Coming. This term itself does not appear until the writings of the church fathers, but the concept is clearly expressed in the New Testament. It is synonymous with "come back" (John 14:3) and "appear a second time" (Hebrews 9:28). In Greek, the term *parousia* ("coming") describes the arrival and presence of a ruler. This term is used frequently to describe the coming of Christ, as in Matthew 24:3, 27, 37, 39.

Unveiling. "Unveil" or "uncover" (Greek, *apocalupsis*) is the Greek title for the Book of Revelation (The Apocalypse). It conveys the idea of a glorious revelation or appearing, as in "you eagerly wait for our Lord Jesus Christ to be revealed" (1 Corinthians 1:7) or "when Jesus Christ is revealed" (1 Peter 1:7).

Appearing. This term (Greek, *epiphaino*) means to "bring to light" or "glorious," as in "by the splendor of His coming" (2 Thessalonians 2:8). From this term comes the liturgical season of Epiphany, which refers to the coming of Christ.

Day of the Lord. This term and its corollary, the "Day of Christ," refer to the time of final judgment which culminates with Armageddon. It appears in the Old Testament as "that great and dreadful Day of the Lord" (Malachi 4:5) and is generally thought to be synonymous with the "time of Jacob's trouble" (Jeremiah 30:7, KJV; Daniel 12:1). In the New Testament it is the "great day of [Christ's] wrath" (Revelation 6:17).

TROUBLE AHEAD

The Bible clearly warns us that there is coming a time of trouble or tribulation for the whole world. As the seven-sealed scroll is opened by Christ (symbolized by the Lamb), Revelation 6–19 tells us in advance what to expect. The Scripture says:

> There was a great earthquake. The sun turned black . . . the moon turned blood red, and the stars in the sky fell. . . . The sky receded like a scroll, rolling up, and every mountain and island was removed from its place (Revelation 6:12-14).

That day will be so terrible that the Bible says people will beg to die rather than survive (Revelation 6:16). The Scripture goes on to tell us that as the seven trumpets sounded,

> There came hail and fire mixed with blood. . . . A third of the earth was burned up, a third of the trees were burned up, and all the green grass was burned up. . . . Something like a huge mountain, all ablaze, was thrown into the sea . . . a third of the living creatures in the sea died. . . . A third of the waters turned bitter. . . . A third of the day was without light (Revelation 8:7-12).

If this were not enough, the prophetic record tells us that a great war will develop in which one-third of mankind will die (Revelation 9:15). Even the description of these warring armies defied ancient description: "Out of their mouths came fire, smoke and sulfur. . . . The power . . . was in their mouths . . . their tails were like snakes" (Revelation 9:17-19). It is obvious that the Apostle John had been transported, in the Spirit, down through the canyon of time and the halls of human history to witness something so distant in the future that it was almost beyond description.

Later, the Revelation describes similar disasters associated with the outpouring of the seven bowls of judgment. It all sounded so fantastic when it was first given that it was probably hard to comprehend. But today it sounds all too familiar

COPY 144-150

—modern warfare, guns, bombs, even nuclear explosions—a fireball polluting the water and burning up the surface of the earth. If we are not racing toward this day of the wrath of God, we soon will be.

THE WHORE OF BABYLON

The Book of Revelation speaks at great length in chapters 17–18 about the fall of "Babylon the Great." This kingdom is personified as "the great whore" (Revelation 17:1, KJV) who has seven heads and ten horns and bears the title:

MYSTERY
BABYLON THE GREAT
THE MOTHER OF PROSTITUTES
AND OF THE ABOMINATIONS OF THE EARTH
Revelation 17:5.

This woman is described as "drunk with the blood of the saints ... who bore the testimony of Jesus" (Revelation 17:6). The seven heads are "seven hills on which the woman sits" (Revelation 17:9), and the ten horns are the "ten kings" who are yet to come (Revelation 17:12). The woman herself is "the great city that rules over the kings of the earth" (Revelation 17:18). There can be little doubt that John is talking about Rome, the great city that ruled the world of his own day and under whose authority he had been banished to the Island of Patmos, where he received this revelation.

This is not the ancient Babylon of Iraq, but the center of the great material, economic, and political system of the Last Days. It is defined as the source of the world's wealth and prosperity. It is the place where sailors and merchants go to make their fortunes (Revelation 18:11-19). Yet the final words of judgment against her are: "Fallen! Fallen is Babylon the Great. . . . In one hour your doom has come. . . . All your riches and splendor have vanished. . . . In one hour she has been brought to ruin" (Revelation 18:2, 10, 14, 19). Whatever this final act of judgment may be, it is instantaneous, devastating, and permanent. It certainly sounds like the consequence of a nuclear war. The prophecy even tells of those who watch the "smoke of her burning" from their ships, but they will not go near her for fear of contamination.

IS THERE ANY IDENTITY ON THE CORPSE?

Not only does the Apostle John, the human author of the Revelation, make it clear that he is talking about Rome, so

DANIEL 2+31 ff 7:1ff

Five Kingdoms

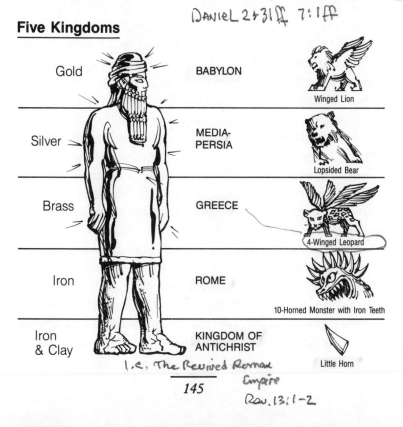

Gold	BABYLON	Winged Lion
Silver	MEDIA-PERSIA	Lopsided Bear
Brass	GREECE	4-Winged Leopard
Iron	ROME	10-Horned Monster with Iron Teeth
Iron & Clay	KINGDOM OF ANTICHRIST	Little Horn

i.e, The Revived Roman Empire

Rev. 13:1-2

does the Old Testament Prophet Daniel. In the days of Nebuchadnezzar, King of ancient Babylon, Daniel was taken captive to Babylon in 605 B.C. There he was forced into a training program for the king's service. He was given a Babylonian name, Belteshazzar, and taught the "language and literature of the Babylonians" (Daniel 1:4). While he was still a student in training, he had an incredible opportunity to interpret the king's dream about a great statue with a head of *gold*, arms of *silver*, belly of *brass*, legs of *iron*, and feet of *iron* and *clay* which was obliterated by a great Rock that filled the whole earth (Daniel 2:31-35).

As Daniel stood before the great Nebuchadnezzar, he told him that God had revealed "what will happen in days to come" (Daniel 2:28). Daniel proceeded to tell Nebuchadnezzar that he was the head of gold and that after him would arise three other kingdoms inferior to his own. Out of the fourth kingdom would come the ten toes, "partly strong and partly brittle" (Daniel 2:42). "In the time of those kings," Daniel explained, "the God of heaven will set up a kingdom that will never be destroyed . . . but it will itself endure forever" (Daniel 2:44). Notice that the supernatural Rock, cut out without hands, fell on the ten toes of the statue.

About fifty years later, in 553 B.C., Daniel himself had a vision (Daniel 7) in which he saw "four great beasts" come up from the sea, also symbolizing these four great empires. What Nebuchadnezzar saw as a beautiful statue, Daniel saw as wild animals about to tear each other apart!

He saw a winged *lion*, the symbol of Babylon. Next came a lopsided *bear*, stronger on one side than the other. He later identified this second kingdom as Media and Persia (Daniel 8:20). The imagery of the two arms of the statue and the lopsided appearance of the bear aptly describes the dual empire which would eventually be dominated by Persia. Next, he saw a four-winged *leopard*, which he later identified as Greece (Daniel 8:21). Finally, he saw a *fourth beast* with ten horns (Daniel 7:7). Its teeth were iron, the same metal as the fourth kingdom in the statue, and it subdued "whatever was left."

While this fourth beast is never identified by Daniel, it is obviously Rome, the empire that succeeded Greece. The statue's two legs (Daniel 2:33) seem to indicate the division of Rome into East (Greek-speaking Constantinople) and West (Latin-speaking Rome). The ten horns of this beast parallel the ten toes of the statue vision (Daniel 2:39-43). They are identified as "ten kings who will come from this kingdom" (Daniel 7:24), after whom will arise "another king," number 11, who will blaspheme God and persecute the saints. Many biblical scholars interpret this person to be the Antichrist.

HORNED-TOED MONSTERS

Evangelical scholars generally interpret the ten horns of Daniel's fourth beast and the ten toes of the statue as being synonymous. Both grow out of the fourth empire and represent the final phase of it. Amillennialists and postmillennialists generally interpret the Rock falling as the *first* coming of Christ, that He established His kingdom (the church) back in the days when Rome ruled the world. By contrast, premillennialists see a gap of time, the Church Age, between the legs and the toes, with the Stone falling at the *second* coming of Christ, during the final stage of Gentile history.

In the statue vision, the Stone fell on the ten toes and obliterated the statue to dust, the wind blew the dust away, and the Stone filled the whole earth. Premillennialists argue that this has never really happened and will only be fulfilled when Christ returns to set up His kingdom on earth during the Millennium (His 1,000-year reign).

In the meantime, attempts to identify the ten horned-toed kings in Roman history have proven futile. Daniel's vision of the four beasts clearly dates them at the end of time. The "little" horn who rises out of the ten horns (Daniel 7:7-8) is said to continue for "a time (one), times (two) and half a time" (Daniel 8:25), or three and one-half times. This is the same time given for the persecution of the "woman" by the Beast in the Apocalypse (Revelation 12:14; 13:5). This is generally taken as the three and one-half years or forty-two months of the Great Tribulation (the last half of seven years of tribulation).

Start Here

WHEN WILL THIS HAPPEN?

Daniel's prophecy of the seventy weeks (Daniel 9) tells us that God put Israel's future on a time clock. God told Daniel that "seventy sevens [weeks, KJV] are decreed for your people [Israel] and your holy city [Jerusalem] to finish transgression, to put an end to sin, to atone for wickedness, to bring in everlasting righteousness, to seal up vision and prophecy, and to anoint the Most Holy" (Daniel 9:24).

The prophecy goes on to predict that seven "sevens" will pass as Jerusalem is rebuilt and sixty-two more "sevens" will pass, for a total of sixty-nine, until the Anointed One (Messiah) will be cut off. This leaves one "seven" left for the future. Biblical scholars have generally taken these "sevens" (Hebrew, *shabua*) to refer to units of seven years; thus, seventy sevens would equal 490 years. By means of simple calculation, from the time of Artaxerxes' decree to rebuild Jerusalem until the Messiah would be cut off would be 483 years (69 "sevens"). That would bring the Jewish calendar to A.D. 32, the year of Christ's crucifixion.[3]

The Jewish calendar was composed of 360 days or twelve months of 30 days. This is the same computation used to calculate three and one-half years as 42 months or 1,260 days (Revelation 12:6-14). Following this calendar, scholars have calculated the *beginning date* of the Persian Emperor Artaxerxes' decree to send Nehemiah to rebuild the city of Jerusalem (Nehemiah 2:1-9) as Nisan 1 (Jewish calendar) or March 14, 445 B.C. The terminal date would be Nisan 10 (Jewish calendar) or April 6, A.D. 32.

The interval between the decree of Artaxerxes and the triumphal entry of Christ at Jerusalem was exactly 173,880 days (or 7 X 69 prophetic years of 360 days each). Reckoning the days inclusively according to Jewish practice, Sir Robert Anderson was the first to work out this computation, and it has been followed by most premillennial scholars.[4] According to Anderson, the 69 weeks of seven years (483 years) terminated on the Sunday our Lord entered Jerusalem in His triumphal entry; that initiated His final rejection by the Jews, which led to His crucifixion ("cut off," Daniel 9:26).

DANIEL'S SEVENTIETH WEEK

This leaves one "week" or unit of seven years yet to come. Dispensational premillennialists find this final seven years in the Tribulation Period, which shall come after the Rapture of the church. During these final seven years, God's prophetic clock for Israel shall begin to tick again.

Notice that the prophecy of the "seventy sevens" was given to Daniel in regard to his people (the Jews) and their holy city (Jerusalem). All of the 490 years have to do with *Israel*, not the church. This focuses our attention on the fact then that Israel plays a prominent role in the Tribulation Period.

In the meantime, Daniel was told, "War will continue until the end" (Daniel 9:26). This is the very same thing Jesus said in the Olivet Discourse (Matthew 24:6). Thus, we can conclude that the "times of the Gentiles" will be marked by wars and by the rise and fall of the four major empires that are to come.

Then Daniel was told of a ruler ("prince," [Daniel 9:26-28, KJV]) who was yet to come and "destroy the city and the sanctuary." Having made a covenant (peace treaty) with Israel, this ruler will break it in the middle of the seventieth "seven" and turn against Jerusalem and cause "desolation" and "abomination," which Jesus also referred to in His prophetic message (Matthew 24:15).

ABOMINATION OF DESOLATION

After Daniel's time, the Jews returned to Jerusalem and rebuilt the temple under Zerubbabel and rebuilt the city walls under Nehemiah. Then the Old Testament revelation closed. For nearly 400 "silent years," there was no new revelation from God. Malachi had predicted Elijah would come again to turn the hearts of the people back to God (Malachi 4:5). Several prophets had pointed to the coming of the Anointed One (Messiah). But as the Old Testament closes, one is left waiting for these promises to be fulfilled.

During the Intertestamental Period (the "silent years"), the Jews were persecuted terribly by the Seleucida ruler, Antiochus IV Epiphanes. In 168 B.C. he vented his wrath on the Jews, as predicted by Daniel, and desecrated the temple, offering a pig on the holy altar! (Daniel 11:21-35) Certainly, this was an abomination to the Jews (Daniel 11:31), but it came *before* the Messiah ever arrived. The Jews revolted under the leadership of Judas Maccabeaus, whose family fought the army of Antiochus from 168 to 165 B.C. Their exploits are recorded in the apocryphal books of 1 and 2 Maccabees. After three years of fighting, they were able to restore worship in Jerusalem and cleansed the temple with a great Feast of Dedication (Hanukkah) on December 25, 165 B.C.[5]

Eventually the Romans conquered Jerusalem and installed Herod the Great as a puppet king under their authority. In an attempt to appease the Jews, Herod had the temple remodeled and greatly expanded. The initial work took about ten years, but construction continued from 20 B.C. to A.D. 64. The edifice was a magnificent sight! Jesus' own disciples were so impressed with it that they wanted to show it off to Him. But our Lord shocked them when He predicted that it would be destroyed and not one stone of it would be left standing (Matthew 24:1-2).

When the Jews revolted against Rome in A.D. 66, the angry Romans retaliated by destroying the temple and burning Jerusalem to the ground. The devastation was accomplished in A.D. 70 by Titus, son of Emperor Vespasian. The population of the city was either slaughtered or enslaved. A subsequent revolt in A.D. 135, led by Jesus Barkokhba, a Jewish zealot, also failed. This time Hadrian plowed under the rubble of the city and erected a Roman city, Aelia Capitolina, from which all Jews were banned. Certainly, this was another "abomination" and "desolation."[6]

Over the centuries that followed, either the Romans, the Arabs, or the Crusaders held Jerusalem. The temple has not been rebuilt and the Jews were scattered in the Great Dispersion (*Diaspora*).[7]

Yet Daniel's prophecy looks all the way down the corridor of time "until the end" (Daniel 9:27). He tells us that there is one great abomination of desolation still on the horizon of the future.

YOU CAN'T TELL THE PLAYERS
WITHOUT A SCORECARD

The key to interpreting the prophecies of the end times is found in Revelation 12–13, where seven symbolic people appear. The identity of these people tells us who the major players are in the Book of Revelation.

1. Woman: Israel (Revelation 12:1-2, 13-16)
The identity of the woman "clothed with the sun ... and a crown of twelve stars on her head" is the most critical issue in properly interpreting the Apocalypse. The Puritans saw her as the church driven into the wilderness (Revelation 12:14) by the Roman papacy. They viewed her as the true church in contrast to the "harlot of Babylon." However, this woman is pregnant with "a male Child [Jesus Christ], who will rule all the nations" (Revelation 12:5). The church did not bring forth Christ; rather, Christ gave birth to the church. The woman here symbolizes Israel because Christ was born of the seed of Israel.

Throughout this chapter the woman, the mother of Christ, is persecuted and driven into the wilderness for 1,260 days or 3½ years (Revelation 12:6, 14) and suffers Great Tribulation, the "time of Jacob's [Israel's] trouble." Amillennialists who see no future for national Israel are forced to view the woman as the church, but she is not. She is the mother (Israel) of Christ, not the bride of Christ (church).

2. Dragon: Satan (Revelation 12:3-4; 9-13)
The "enormous red dragon with seven heads and ten horns" (Revelation 12:3) is identified as "the devil or Satan" (Revelation 12:9). He is called the "accuser of our brothers, who accuses them before our God day and night." The language is reminiscent of the story of Satan's activity in the Book of

Job. Satan is also described as the one who tried to devour the Child as soon as it was born. The whole passage reminds us of the great spiritual warfare going on behind the scenes of human history.

3. *Male Child: Christ* (Revelation 12:2, 5)
The Child is obviously Jesus Christ, who will "rule all the nations with an iron scepter" (Revelation 12:5). His being "snatched up" to the throne of God refers to Christ's ascension back to heaven (Acts 1:10-11). Jesus is symbolized by the Lamb in Revelation 5, 14, 19, 21–22.[8] He is the One who opens the seven-sealed scroll, the title deed to the universe. He is the One who gathers His elect and judges the unbelieving world. He is the Bridegroom at the wedding supper. He is the Rider on the white horse who overcomes the Beast, the false prophet, and the dragon and rules forever.

4. *Michael: The Archangel* (Revelation 12:7-12)
In this spectacular prophecy, we are told that Michael and his angels cast Satan out of heaven. Lucifer (or Satan) had already "fallen" from his lofty position, but still had access to the throne of God, as we read in Job 1:6-12; 2:1-7. But now Satan is booted out of heaven completely and is hurled to the earth. He is angry because he knows his time is short (Revelation 12:12), so he vents his anger on the woman (Israel), who had given birth to the Child. His time left is "a time, times and half a time" (3½ years). This time coincides with the last half of Daniel's seventieth week, the Great Tribulation.

5. *The Remnant: Believers* (Revelation 12:17)
When Satan is thwarted in his attempt to destroy national Israel, he turns against the remnant of her seed who have the "testimony of Jesus." These are converted Jews; they have come to faith in Jesus as their Messiah. They are persecuted severely by the two beasts that are forthcoming. Some specu-

late that the deliverance by the "wings of a great eagle" (Revelation 12:14) may refer to an airlift, but that is purely speculation.

6. *Beast of the Sea: Antichrist* (Revelation 13:1-10)
This creature represents the epitome and culmination of the Gentile powers of all time. Thus, he/it resembles a lion, a bear, and a leopard, as in Daniel's vision of the four beasts (Daniel 7). He/it is also symbolized by seven heads and ten horns, as in Daniel's prophecy of the fourth beast, or fourth empire. This creature is said to "blaspheme God," to make "war against the saints," and receive "worship" from unbelievers. The Apostle Paul calls him the "man of lawlessness" (2 Thessalonians 2:3) or "man of sin" (KJV) or "son of perdition" (KJV), who "exalts himself over everything that is called God or is worshiped, and even sets himself up in God's temple, proclaiming himself to be God" (2 Thessalonians 2:4).

Most commentators understand the Beast of the sea to be the Antichrist. Whether he is a specific person, political system, or both, is a matter of debate. Since he/it is associated with the same symbolism as Rome (seven heads and ten horns), it is *assumed* that he/it represents the revived Roman Empire of the last days. Some *speculate* that this could be in the process of being formed even now in the European Economic Community (EEC).

The characteristics of this beast are the same as those of the "little horn" of Daniel's prophecy (Daniel 7:8). He also appears to be the "ruler" or "prince" (KJV) that shall come to bring the final abomination of desolation upon Jerusalem.

7. *Beast of the Earth: False Prophet* (Revelation 13:11-18)
This creature is distinct from the Beast of the sea in that he calls attention to the first beast and persuades the world to worship the Antichrist. He even sets up an *image* of the first Beast "so that it could speak" (Revelation 13:15). The spec-

ulative possibilities here are endless. Is this some kind of tel-evised image? Can this telecast work as a two-way response? Is it a projected holographic image that actually appears as a three-dimensional person? At this point in time, no one knows for sure. This second beast is also said to be able to force people to receive the *mark* of the first Beast which is described as a mark (insignia or logo), a number (666), or a name (?) which people must receive in order to "buy or sell."

Whoever or whatever this second beast is, he/it is able to control the world politically, religiously, and economically during the Tribulation Period. Later, when these two are con-quered by Jesus Christ and cast into the lake of fire, they are called the "beast" and the "false prophet" (Revelation 19:20). Many take these two to be the one-world government and the one-world religion of the last days.

HOW CAN WE BE SURE?

Since much of the interpretation of prophecy rests on the symbolism of Daniel and Revelation, we need to be cautious about *assuming* our own views are right and then *speculating* way beyond what the Scripture actually states as *fact*.

We all would like to think that our view is the correct view of prophecy, but we must remember that genuine believers differ on matters of eschatology. When we stoop to con-demning them for being different or even attacking their character and sincerity, we are really admitting our own inse-curity about our own position. The easiest way to avoid dis-cussing the issues is to attack your opponent.

Tragically, eschatology has become a divisive issue among evangelicals. In some circles, any variation from commonly held views results in immediate expulsion, ostracism, and de-nunciation. This keeps the church leaders from any healthy discussion about the end times or evaluation of other eschatological options. For this reason there has come a great stagnation in the whole area of eschatology in recent years. What is worse, some people are completely unaware of other options and keep preaching what they have been taught as though it were fact.

As a premillennialist I have certain prejudices of my own about eschatology. I believe the postmillennial dream of bringing in the kingdom of Christ on earth during the Church Age is a futile enterprise. But that does not mean that postmillennialists are bad people or that they should not be commended for their concern to make an impact on society. Jonathan Edwards, the Puritan revivalist, was a postmillennialist, and he is revered in all evangelical circles. So are great postmillennial theologians like Charles Hodge and Benjamin Warfield.

I believe amillennialists fail to distinguish between Israel and the church and they allegorize away the prediction of a thousand-year kingdom on earth. But this does not make them Christ-denying heretics. They are to be commended for their concern that the church fulfill its responsibilities on earth and prepare men and women for the judgment to come. Prominent amillennialists include television pastor D. James Kennedy, founder of Evangelism Explosion, and biblical counseling advocate Jay Adams. Both of these men have made great contributions to the cause of the evangelical faith, as have amillennial scholars such as William Hendriksen and Anthony Hoekema.

American Christianity has a rich, varied heritage of eschatological teaching that is virtually absent in England, continental Europe, and other parts of the world. We have an opportunity to benefit from each other's perspective if we are willing to discuss and evaluate our beliefs based upon the *facts* of prophetic Scripture.

9

WHAT IS NEXT?

My children and I were paddling late one summer afternoon across the crystal waters of one of Michigan's northern lakes. As the sun dipped toward the horizon, it appeared larger and larger. Then dramatically, it dropped below the distant surface of the lake. Suddenly the light paled and darkness began to fall.

It was as though the sun had fallen out of the sky never to rise again. It was one of those unforgettable moments that leaves you all alone with the stark realities of nature.

"Will it come back?" my youngest asked, knowing it would, but wanting assurance from someone older.

"Yes, Jon," I replied. "It will be back tomorrow."

As we paddled back to shore, I remember thinking that there would eventually come a time when that assurance couldn't be given. The Book of Revelation tells us there is a time coming when the sun and moon will not shine, the stars will fall, and the world will be plunged into darkness.

SPIRITUAL APOSTASY

One of the great warnings of prophetic Scripture is that false teaching will bring deception upon professing Christendom in the Last Days. Jesus Himself warned that "*many* will come in My name, claiming, 'I am the Christ,' and will deceive *many*" (Matthew 24:5, italics added). He also predicted that "*many* false prophets will appear and deceive *many* people" (Matthew 24:11, italics added).

Our Lord indicated this would continue throughout the Church Age, but He also spoke of a time of "Great Tribulation" (KJV), at the end of the age in which false messiahs and false prophets would perform miracles to deceive the public and even confuse the elect.

The Apostle Paul predicted, "There will be terrible times in the last days" in which people would become materialistic, self-centered, abusive, disobedient, ungrateful, unforgiving, and unholy (2 Timothy 3:1-3). Paul said this generation would be "lovers of pleasure rather than lovers of God" (2 Timothy 3:4).

Peter predicted that "in the last days scoffers will come, scoffing and following their own evil desires" (2 Peter 3:3). These unbelievers will deny the second coming of Christ, saying, "Where is this 'coming' He promised?" (2 Peter 3:4) Jude quotes Peter and adds these men "follow mere natural instincts and do not have the Spirit" (Jude 19).

We should not be surprised, therefore, with the great spiritual confusion that abounds even now: Liberal theologians suggesting that there will be no literal return of Christ; Jehovah's Witnesses claiming He has already come secretly in 1914; Mormons telling us they are the only true "Latter Day Saints"; the Unification Church ("Moonies") affirming that Sun Myung Moon is the Messiah; *ad infinitum, ad nauseum!*

THE CLOUDS
OF SECULARISM

Historian Paul Johnson has called the twentieth century *Modern Times*.[1] Certainly, this century has brought the most incredible changes imaginable to the human race: automobiles, airplanes, radios, televisions, computers, and a host of other gadgets which have shaped our lives in ways our forefathers could never have imagined.

Yet with the advancement of modernity has come a restless uneasiness about the spiritual and traditional values of our culture which are fast slipping away. At times consciously and at other times unconsciously, we seem to be discarding the very ideas that made America great.[2]

Charles Colson opens his book *Against the Night* with the observation: "We sense that things are winding down.... Our great civilization may not yet lie in smoldering ruins, but the enemy is within the gates. The times seem to smell of sunset."[3]

Throughout the twentieth century, secularism replaced the Judeo-Christian values of our society. God was gradually and systematically removed from any place of prominence in our culture and our intellectual lives. Scientism turned science into a religion which taught that natural laws, not spiritual principles, guide the universe. The entrenchment of the theory of evolution in our schools made God irrelevant to our culture. Men now see themselves as little more than glorified animals whose highest instinct is self-gratification.

We should not be surprised then when educators, sociologists, psychologists, and other assessors of life tell us that ours is a self-centered culture.[4] The self-indulgent pursuit of money, power, and fame has plunged our whole society down the toboggan slide of narcissism.

HAVE WE LOST OUR MINDS?

Joining hands with secularism is the philosophical concept of *relativism*, which teaches that there is no absolute truth. Something is only viewed as being true because a group of people accept it as true. Relativism dethrones all absolutes, including God and His laws. The great danger of this concept is that it leads to a naive acceptance of secularism. Nothing is viewed as right or wrong in itself, but only as it relates to its context.

The influence of relativism has affected nearly every area of our culture. One of the most powerful books to appear in the 1980s was Allan Bloom's *The Closing of the American Mind*, which explored the intellectual vacuum of our time.[5] He argues that today's students are unlike any generation that has preceded them because they have been robbed of truth and dignity by the philosophy of relativism which permeates higher education.

"Today's students are no longer interested in noble causes," Bloom bemoans. "There is an indifference to such things for relativism has extinguished the real motive of education."[6] He observes that today's students have generally abandoned themselves to the pursuit of the good life or what Arthur Levine called "going first class on the Titanic."[7]

THE APPEASEMENT OF EVIL

The greatest danger of relativism is that it leads to the appeasement of evil. If all truth is relative, then all ethics are situational. If I have part of the truth and you have part of the truth, then neither of us has the whole truth. Once we accept this concept, we have no basis on which to judge any action as morally right or wrong.

The unborn, the elderly, the retarded, and the handicapped all become expendable by such logic. We should not be surprised that secular society is willing to tolerate abortion, euthanasia, and even infanticide. And it will not be long until that same logic will be used to suggest the elimination of those who oppose what is best for the good of the new world order.

Former Surgeon General C. Everett Koop called this indifference to the sanctity of life the "slide to Auschwitz." It is the same intellectual journey that led to Hitler's Nazi atrocities under the guise of helping the evolutionary process of natural selection eliminate undesirable life forms.

NEW AGE MYSTICISM

Relativism also opens the door to mysticism. Modern man has reached a point where he really doesn't want to face the logical consequences of a secular world without God, so he is turning to a kind of scientific mysticism popularized as the New Age movement.[8]

New Age thinking is a do-it-yourself religion with a smorgasbord of options: spiritism, witchcraft, channeling, transcendentalism, Oriental mysticism, and transpersonal psychology. Intellectually, it grows out of the belief that the world is now evolving spiritually, producing a great "planetary consciousness" that will eventually lead to a new world order.

New Agers are calling for the total transformation of society along social and political lines consistent with their own beliefs. They see mankind emerging into human consciousness and human potential by declaring its own deification, leaving God "watching from a distance," as the top song of 1990 put it ("From a Distance," sung by Bette Middler).

THE GREAT
BRAIN ROBBERY

It has been nearly thirty years now since Francis Schaeffer argued that the rationalism of our secular society would eventually rob our culture of its rationality.[9] He was right! We are now reaping the consequences of a world gone mad intellectually. Feelings have replaced truth as the benchmark of our culture. "If it feels good, do it" was a slogan in the 1970s, but it is the reality of everyday life in the '90s.

As we rapidly approach the end of the century and the dawn of the third millennium of church history, it is clear that the mindset of our society is shifting dramatically. While we cannot predict that current intellectual trends will necessarily lead to the deception of the Last Days of which Scripture warns, it would certainly seem that the trend is not in our favor. Undoubtedly, the intellectual deck is stacked against us in the battle for the minds of men.

The intellectual bankruptcy of our culture is indeed the great brain robbery of our times. Now, with Eastern Europe, the Soviet Union, and even parts of the Arab world opening up to Western culture, what have we to offer them other than the material goods of our indulgent society? Most of what we send them will only trap them in the same mindless pursuit of self-indulgence in which we ourselves are caught.

Whether the final deception of the end times stems directly from the intellectual developments of our own time remains to be seen. What is clear is that the Christian consensus that once dominated Western culture is now shattered and is unlikely to be recovered. The world is already mired in the quicksands of secularism, relativism, and mysticism. Has the great deception already begun?

RAPTURE OF THE CHURCH

The hope of the church is the return of Jesus Christ. She does not await the end of the world in the same sense that the rest of the world does. Rene Pache said: "The signs of the times warn her that her deliverance is near; the sufferings here below, the last assaults of the enemy, cause her to say ever more ardently, 'Lord Jesus, come quickly!'"[10]

The church awaits a Person, not destruction. Peter explains that the present world is "reserved for fire, being kept for the day of judgment and destruction of *ungodly* men" (2 Peter 3:7, italics mine). While the church is told to prepare for suffering and persecution throughout the Church Age, she is *not* pictured in Scripture as the object of God's final wrath. In fact, our Lord said to the church, "I will also keep you from the hour of trial that is going to come upon the whole world" (Revelation 3:10). Notice, the church is to be kept *from* (literally, "out of"), not *through*, the hour of trouble that is coming.

The Rapture (or translation) of the church is often paralleled to the "raptures" of Enoch (Genesis 5:24) and Elijah (2 Kings 2:12) or the ascension of Christ (Acts 1:9), all of whom were "taken up" into heaven. The Bible clearly states: "For the Lord Himself will come down from heaven, with a loud command, with the voice of the archangel and with the trumpet call of God, and the dead in Christ will rise first. After that, we who are still alive and are left will be *caught up* with them in the clouds to meet the Lord in the air. And so we will be with the Lord forever" (1 Thessalonians 4:16-17, italics added).

The Rapture will take *up* both those who have died in Christ over the centuries and those alive when He returns. This is the time our Lord spoke of when He said, "A time is coming when all who are in their graves will hear His voice and come out" (John 5:28). Believers are pictured as being raised to *life* (the first resurrection) and unbelievers as being raised to *judgment* (the second resurrection). Of the resurrection of believers, the Bible says, "They came to life and reigned with Christ a thousand years. . . . This is the first resurrection" (Revelation 20:4-5). Of the unbelievers, the Scripture says, "The rest of the dead did not come to life until the thousand years were ended" (Revelation 20:5).

WHEN WILL THE RAPTURE OCCUR?

The *fact* that there will be a Rapture is clearly taught in Scripture. The real debate is over *when* it will occur. *Pre-Tribulationists* believe the church will be raised before the Tribulation Period.[11] *Mid-Tribulationists* believe the church will enter the Tribulation and be raptured at some midpoint during it.[12] *Post-Tribulationists* believe the church will go through the Tribulation as the suffering "saints" of Revelation. They view the Rapture as coming at the end of the Tribulation.[13]

Let me suggest several reasons why I believe the Rapture will occur *before* the Tribulation Period.

1. *Christ promised to keep the church from the Tribulation.* In Revelation 3:10, the risen Christ said the church would be *kept from* (literally, "preserved" or "protected *out* of") the hour of trial that is coming on the whole world. This is no local judgment or persecution in view, but a worldwide judgment of God. The events described in the Apocalypse are acts of divine retribution. They are not merely human persecutions.

2. *The judgments of the Tribulation Period are called the "wrath of the Lamb."* Revelation 6:16 depicts the cataclysmic judgments of the end times as the wrath of Christ, the Lamb

of God. The Book of Revelation also depicts the church as the bride of the Lamb (Revelation 19:7-9). She is not the object of His wrath against unbelievers. Nor is it likely He will condemn the church, which He is going to marry, with the rest of the world. He may purge her to cleanse her, but He will not judge her for unbelief.

3. *Jesus told His disciples to pray they would escape the Tribulation.* In Luke 21:36 He said: "Be always on the watch, and pray that you may be able to escape all that is about to happen, and that you may be able to stand before the Son of man." Remember, even Lot was given a chance to escape Sodom before divine judgment fell (cf. Genesis 19; Luke 17:28-36).

4. *His coming in the clouds means the church's deliverance has come.* Jesus told His disciples that when He comes in the clouds, "stand up and lift up your heads, because your redemption is drawing near" (Luke 21:28). The hope of the church is not surviving the Tribulation but escaping it.

5. *God will call His ambassadors home before declaring war on the world.* In 2 Corinthians 5:20, believers are called "Christ's ambassadors" who appeal to the world to be reconciled to God. God will recall His ambassadors at the Rapture before He unleashes His final judgments on the unbelieving world.

6. *Moral restraint will disappear when the church is taken.* Paul's words, in 2 Thessalonians 2:1-11, refer to the "coming of our Lord" and "our being gathered to Him." These verses also warn that the "man of lawlessness" (Antichrist) will be revealed only *after* the restraining power of God is removed from the world. While some assume this is the Holy Spirit who indwells the church, it would seem more likely that it is the church itself that is removed. Her "salt and light" ministry of restraining evil in the world will have been completed, whereas the omnipresent Holy Spirit will continue His min-

istry even during the Tribulation Period, during which time a host of Jews and Gentiles will be converted to faith in Christ (Revelation 7:9-14).

7. *The Rapture will happen in the "twinkling of an eye."* The Bible says, "We will not all sleep [in death], but we will all be changed—in a flash, in the twinkling of an eye, at the last trumpet. For the trumpet will sound, the dead will be raised imperishable, and we [those living at the Rapture] will be changed" (1 Corinthians 15:51-52). This instantaneous disappearance will terminate the church's earthly ministry.

8. *The Rapture will take place in the air.* The Bible states that we who are alive on earth at the time of the Rapture will be "caught up . . . to meet the Lord in the air" (1 Thessalonians 4:17). This is quite in contrast to our Lord's coming *with* His saints when He returns to the earth after the Tribulation. At that time He will split the Mount of Olives. The Prophet Zechariah said: "Then the Lord my God will come, and all the holy ones with Him" (Zechariah 14:5). At the Rapture we go *up* and at the return we come back *down* with Christ.

9. *The woman who suffers persecution during the Tribulation symbolizes Israel.* The woman, Israel, delivers the male Child, or Christ (Revelation 12:1-2, 5-6). Israel as a nation brought forth Christ; He then established the church. Since He is its founder and not its descendant, the woman cannot be the church. This symbolism clearly indicates that Israel, not the church, will suffer. The church is absent, already having been raptured.

10. *The Marriage of Christ (the Lamb) and His bride (the church) takes place before the Battle of Armageddon.* The Scripture describes the fall of the kingdom of Antichrist (symbolically called "Babylon") in Revelation 17–18. But *before* it tells of Christ's returning from heaven on the white horse to conquer the Beast and the false prophet (Revelation

19:11-21), it tells us "the wedding of the Lamb has come, and His bride has made herself ready" (Revelation 19:7-8). This clearly indicates the bride has been taken to heaven earlier and that she returns with Christ in the host of the "armies of heaven . . . riding on white horses and dressed in fine linen, white and clean" (cf. Revelation 19:8, 14).

THE GREAT TRIBULATION

The Old Testament prophets called it the "Day of the Lord" (Joel 1:15) or the "day of vengeance of our God" (Isaiah 61:2). They described it as a day of darkness (Amos 5:18); and of fire (Zephaniah 1:18); burning as hot as a furnace (Malachi 4:1). "That day will be a day of wrath, a day of distress and anguish, a day of trouble and ruin, a day of darkness and gloom . . . because they have sinned against the Lord" (Zephaniah 1:15-17). This day of divine judgment against unbelievers will consume the whole world (Zephaniah 1:18).

The Old Testament closes with the warning of the coming of the Day of the Lord (Malachi 4). Yet it promises hope for those who revere His name. These will "go out and leap" for joy. Malachi also promised that before that "great and dreadful day," the Prophet Elijah would return, which Jesus said was fulfilled in the coming of John the Baptist (Matthew 11:14).

The Great Tribulation is the period of divine judgment which immediately precedes the coming of Christ in power and great glory. The Prophet Ezekiel called it: "The Day of the Lord . . . a day of clouds, a time of doom for the nations [Gentiles]" (Ezekiel 30:3). He even named many of those nations: Egypt, Cush, Put, Lydia, Arabia, and Libya (Ezekiel 30:5).

In recent years it has been customary for pre-Tribulation-ists to see two great battles coming in the future:

- Magog and her Arab allies against Israel.
- Antichrist and his kingdom against Israel.

Older pre-Tribulationists, like Rene Pache, viewed this as one great end-time battle, noting that many of the same nations are named as falling on the "Day of the Lord" (Armageddon) in Ezekiel 30:1-8. However one interprets these end-time conflicts, the Bible clearly teaches that Israel, not the church, is the target of these attacks and that in the final battle Christ will return with His church saints, His bride, to deliver Israel and complete the unity of God's people.

The final battle of Armageddon is called the:

- Wrath of the Lord (Isaiah 26:20).
- Hot anger of the Lord (Ezekiel 38:18).
- Dread of the Lord (Isaiah 2:10).
- Vengeance of God (Isaiah 35:4).
- Harvest of Judgment (Micah 4:11-12; Revelation 14:14-20).
- Grapes of Wrath (Isaiah 63:1-6; Revelation 19:15).
- Great Banquet of God (Ezekiel 39:17-20; Revelation 19:17-18).

The devastation of Armageddon is so extensive that it is probably best viewed as a *war* which destroys most of the earth, as well as a final *battle* focused in the Middle East. This also best explains the development of events in Revelation 15-19.

The carnage will be so great that most of the earth's population will be annihilated. The vegetation of the planet will be nearly destroyed. The air and water will be severely polluted. "Babylon" will be burned up. The armies of the Antichrist will be annihilated, and the Beast and the false prophet will be thrown into the lake of fire (Revelation 14-19).

The final devastation will be the self-destructive acts of a world gone mad without God. The Bible says:
- Darkness will reign (Isaiah 5:30; Zechariah 14:7).
- Heavens shall be shaken (Isaiah 34:4).
- Earth will quake (Isaiah 29:6; Zechariah 14:4-5).
- Huge hailstones will fall from heaven (Revelation 16:21).
- The invading host will destroy itself (Zechariah 14:13).

The Prophet Zechariah describes this day in vivid terms:

> The Lord will strike all the nations that fought against Jerusalem: Their flesh will rot while they are standing on their feet, their eyes will rot in their sockets, and their tongues will rot in their mouths. On that day men will be stricken by the Lord with great panic. Each man will seize the hand of another, and they will attack each other (Zechariah 14:12-13).

THE MILLENNIAL KINGDOM

As terrible as the Battle of Armageddon will be, it will not mark the end of the earth. Zechariah 14:16 tells us that the "survivors from all the nations that have attacked Jerusalem will go up year after year to worship the King, the Lord Almighty." Revelation 20:1-6 tells us that Satan will be bound a thousand years while we serve as "priests of God and Christ" and will reign with Him for a thousand years.

Premillennialists, in general, interpret this as a time when resurrected and raptured saints rule with Christ over the survivors of the Great Tribulation who live on earth during the Millennium of Christ's earthly rule. This is generally interpreted to be a time of peace and prosperity unparalleled in human history.

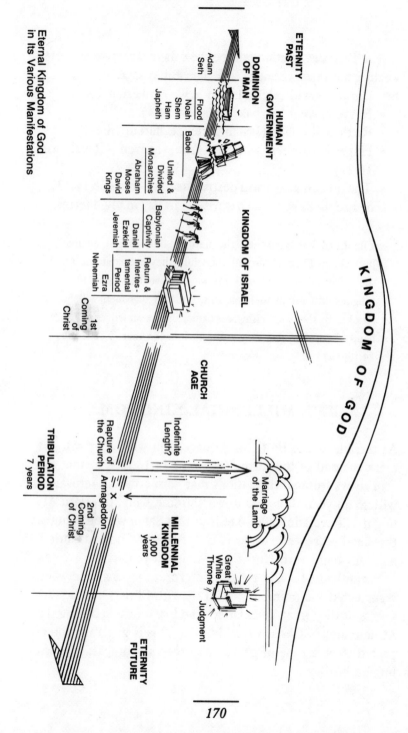

Eternal Kingdom of God in Its Various Manifestations

The kingdom of God is best pictured as being eternal. It began in eternity past and it will extend into the eternal future. It exists wherever God exists and whenever God exists. It has been manifested on earth in the dominion of man and through the means of human government. It was particularly manifested in the kingdom of Israel from the call of Abraham through the conquest of Canaan by Joshua and from the establishment of the throne of David until the Babylonian Captivity.

In the New Testament era, the kingdom of God is *spiritual* in nature (Matthew 13). It is "within" the hearts of believers who are its citizens by faith in Christ. Thus, in the Church Age, the kingdom is expressed in our Spirit-empowered relationship to Christ. But during the millennial kingdom, the kingdom of God will be fully visible as Christ visibly reigns on the earth.

But even after the Millennium, the Scripture tells us that fire will destroy this planet (Revelation 20:7-9; 2 Peter 3:10-13). "Everything will be destroyed," Peter tells us. "The heavens by fire, and the elements will melt in the heat." Accordingly, the Bible points to our ultimate destiny: a new heaven and a new earth as the home of the righteous (2 Peter 2:13; Revelation 21–22).

In light of the temporary nature of our present material world, the Scripture urges us to live "holy and godly lives" and to be "found spotless, blameless and at peace" with God (2 Peter 3:11, 14). This earth is not our final destiny. We are just pilgrims passing through on our way to our eternal home.

10

IT ISN'T OVER
TILL IT'S OVER

One of the great baseball minds of all time, Yogi Bera, used to say, "It ain't over till it's over!" He was referring to the unpredictable endings in athletic events. Just when the ball game appears to be down to the last easy, predictable out, anything and everything can start happening.

That is about how it is in trying to relate current events to Bible prophecy. About the time you think you have it all figured out, something unexpected happens. Nobody was prepared for the sudden and spontaneous collapse of communism in Eastern Europe. I cannot think of one prophetic writer who anticipated such an event happening so quickly. Nobody, other than the Israelis, took Saddam Hussein seriously. Prophetic speculators warned us about Iran, Egypt, and Libya, but hardly anyone talked about Iraq, and most people had never even heard of Kuwait.

As incomprehensible as it seems, some of the world's greatest crises have been precipitated in some of the most obscure places: the assassination of the Austrian archduke in Sarajevo, Yugoslavia, was the spark that ignited World War I;

the German invasion of Czechoslovakia began the chain of events that led to World War II; the remote jungles of Vietnam took away American pride and confidence; and the invasion of the tiny kingdom of Kuwait brought about the greatest mobilization of military forces since World War II.

It makes one wonder how it will all end someday. Perhaps in some obscure outpost of humanity, the spark will be lit that leads to Armageddon. It may even seem insignificant at first, but then, like the beginnings of a great conflagration, the flames of hatred quickly spread out of control and the world will find itself on the verge of extinction.

WHERE WILL IT ALL END?

The Bible warns us that humanity is marching in a death cadence to inevitable destruction. It may not come now or even in our lifetimes, but one day the end will come. When it does, the Scripture tells us that the great crisis will begin in the Middle East and spread to the whole world.

The Prophet Isaiah warned of a time coming when God would judge the whole earth (Isaiah 24).[1] He foresaw a time when God would "lay waste the earth and devastate it. . . . The earth will be completely laid waste and totally plundered. . . . The earth dries up and withers, the world languishes. . . . earth's inhabitants are burned up, and very few are left" (Isaiah 24:1-6).

There can be little doubt that Isaiah is talking about the Great Tribulation that culminates in the Battle of Armageddon.[2] He sees a world in which God's wrath is being poured on "all nations" (Isaiah 34:2) and where the "mountains shall be melted" (Isaiah 34:3, KJV) and the "stars of heaven will be dissolved and the sky rolled up like a scroll" (Isaiah 34:4).

In both Isaiah 24 and 34, the prophet sees ahead to the

time of God's judgment on the whole world. While the Scripture records specific judgments on Israel during the "time of Jacob's trouble" and upon the coalition kingdom of the Antichrist, symbolically called "Babylon," it also tells us that an even greater judgment will come upon the world at large. Virtually no person or place shall escape God's retribution at the end time. This apocalyptic holocaust will be worldwide and almost no one will be spared.

HOW WILL IT ALL END?

The question of *how* this will all come about divides evangelicals according to their eschatological views. *Pre-Tribulationists* believe that Christ will rapture the church to heaven prior to the Great Tribulation and then return with His bride at the end of the Tribulation to set of His kingdom on earth. *Mid-* and *post-Tribulationists* believe the church will suffer to some extent during the Tribulation Period and be caught up at a midpoint or at the very end of the Great Tribulation.

Amillennialists believe that things will get worse at the end of the Church Age. While most view the entire Church Age as a time of tribulation for believers, many feel that the persecution of the saints (Christians) will get worse in the "Last Days." At the very end, the Battle of Armageddon will commence and Christ will return to judge the world and usher in eternity.

Postmillennialists believe that the church is the kingdom of God on earth and that it is our responsibility to bring in the kingdom by the preaching of the Gospel and the enactment of Christian laws, values, and principles in society until the whole world is converted to Christ.

Obviously, there are great differences in each of these views and yet each one contains an element of truth that all

Christians need to remember. From the *pre-Tribulationalist* we are reminded to be ready for the coming of Christ at any moment. From the *mid-* and *post-Tribulationist* we are reminded that many times Christians are called to suffer for their Lord. Certainly, believers in the Third World could teach us much about what it means to suffer for Christ.

The *amillennialist* reminds us all that we must be ready to face the judgment of God. While it is exciting to think about our Lord's coming, we must also realize that His judgment is coming as well. While we premillennialists look forward to Christ's earthly kingdom, we must also remember that even that will come to an end and be merged into eternity into the eternal kingdom of God. The Apostle Paul reminds us there is coming a time when Christ "hands over the kingdom to God the Father" (1 Corinthians 15:24).

From the *postmillennialist* we are reminded of our Christian responsibilities to the world in which we live. Since we do not know the exact time of Christ's return, we dare not sit back and do nothing but wait for the Rapture. Christ has given us very specific orders about our responsibilities to one another and to the world at large. We are called to be the light of the world and the salt of the earth until our Lord returns (Matthew 5:13-16).

WHEN WILL IT ALL END?

The Bible makes it clear that no one but God knows the exact time of the end of the age (Matthew 24:36). Therefore, even the most sincerely calculated guesses are destined to fail. The clues given in Scripture are these:

1. *When the Gospel has been preached to the whole world,* "then the end will come" (Matthew 24:14). This indicates our mandate to continue evangelizing until Jesus comes again.

2. *When the bride of Christ (the church) is complete* and the last convert has been added, Christ will come for His church. Jesus said, "I go and prepare a place for you, I will come back and take you to be with Me that you also may be where I am" (John 14:2-3).

3. *When the church is raptured to heaven,* the Church Age will close. Paul said, "We who are still alive and are left will be caught up with them in the clouds to meet the Lord in the air. And so we will be with the Lord forever" (1 Thessalonians 4:17).

4. *When the "times of the Gentiles" have been completed,* God again will deal with Israel as His people on earth. Jesus said to His disciples, "Jerusalem will be trampled on by the Gentiles until the times of the Gentiles are fulfilled" (Luke 21:24).

5. *When the marriage of Christ and the church is finalized,* believers will be in a perfect and fixed moral state for all eternity. In the present era, the church is engaged to Christ (2 Corinthians 11:2) in a relationship that is so binding it is described as marriage (Romans 7:2-4). But after the Rapture, the bride will be made ready for the marriage supper in heaven (Revelation 19:1-7).

WHAT SHOULD WE BE DOING?

Since we can never be sure when God's purposes for His church will be finalized, we must remain obedient to our Lord's commands regarding His church. This was made clear to the disciples at the time of Christ's ascension to heaven. They had asked if He were going to restore the kingdom to Israel at that time, and Jesus told them, "It is not for you to know the times or dates the Father has set by His own authority" (Acts 1:7). Two things are obvious from this statement: (1) The date has been set; (2) We aren't supposed to know it because we have a responsibility to fulfill in the meantime.

In the very next verse, Jesus gave the Great Commission, telling them they would be empowered by the Holy Spirit to be His witnesses in Jerusalem, Judea, Samaria, and unto the "ends of the earth" (Acts 1:8). Then, to their amazement, He ascended into heaven, leaving them gazing intently into the sky. Then two men in white (probably angels) appeared and asked, "Why do you stand here looking into the sky? This same Jesus, who has been taken from you into heaven, will come back in the same way you have seen Him go into heaven" (Acts 1:11).

All too often, today's Christians are just like those early disciples. We spend more time gazing into the sky and speculating about Christ's return than we actually spend serving Him. The angels' point was to remind them that His return is certain. Don't waste time and energy worrying about when or whether Christ will return. Believe that He is coming again on schedule and be about His business in the meantime.

Jesus left several instructions about what we ought to be doing in the meantime:

1. *Witness for Him everywhere you go.* Our Lord told His disciples to be His witnesses everywhere they might go, even to the farthest ends of the earth (Acts 1:8).

2. *"Go into all the world and preach the good news,"* He also told His disciples (Mark 16:15). This command emphasizes the evangelistic and missionary nature of the church's ministry during the present era. We are to take the Gospel to the whole world.

3. *"Repentance and forgiveness of sins will be preached . . . to all nations,"* our Lord declared in Luke 24:47. Calling men and women to repent and believe the Gospel is the twofold nature of the evangelistic enterprise.

4. *"Make disciples of all nations, baptizing them,"* He said in Matthew 28:19. Making converts and discipling them in their obedient walk with God is also a major emphasis of the church's mission.

5. *Build the church and attack the gates of hell.* Jesus told His disciples that He would build His church with such power that "the gates of hell shall not prevail against it" (Matthew 16:18, KJV). We usually picture this as though hell were attacking the church and we were trying to survive. But remember, you don't attack with gates. You defend with gates. Jesus pictured the church on the offensive and hell on the defensive.

6. *"Occupy till I come"* (Luke 19:13, KJV), Jesus said in the Parable of the Talents. He was referring to using the money He mentioned in the parable. The servants were to "put this money to work" until their master returned. We are to stay busy about the Master's business until He returns.

7. *Remain faithful until He returns.* Our Lord concluded His prophetic message in the Olivet Discourse by reminding His disciples to continue in faithful and wise service even though He might be gone a long time (Matthew 24:45-51; 25:14-21).

THE END HAS ALREADY BEGUN

Almost 2,000 years ago, the Apostle Peter said, "The end of all things is near. Therefore be clear minded and self-controlled so that you can pray" (1 Peter 4:7). Way back then Peter and the other apostles of Christ sensed that they had moved dramatically closer to the consummation of God's plan for this world. The Old Testament era had come to an end, and they were now part of a new era under the New Testament.

Peter's reference to the end is expressed by a verb in the perfect tense in the original Greek. This means the action involved is a present reality with future consequences. It could just as appropriately be translated, "The end of all things has already begun." For Peter, the end of the age was already a present reality.

The first coming of Christ initiated the end of the age (see Acts 2:14-20 and Hebrews 1:2) and His second coming will terminate the end of the age (Matthew 24:30). Therefore, the entire Church Age is a Last Days in a general sense. Whereas, the very end of those days is a specific Last Days, or a last of the Last Days.

The Scripture also speaks of the end as a future event. The Apostle Paul predicted, "There will be terrible times in the Last Days" (2 Timothy 3:1). The opening verse of the Apocalypse refers to "things which must shortly come to pass" (Revelation 1:1, KJV) and goes on to warn us that "the time is near" (Revelation 1:3). The Scripture also presents Christ's coming as an imminent reality. "Behold, I am coming soon," Christ promised (Revelation 22:7). He will come suddenly, and He could come at any moment.

The ominous events of the recent Persian Gulf War remind us all of how quickly an international crisis of great magnitude can erupt in the Middle East. While other conflicts may come and go, the Bible focuses on the Middle East as the place where the ultimate conflict will come.

WHAT TIME IS IT?

This leaves us asking the question: What time is it now? Peter referred to the *present* saying, "[Christ] was revealed in these last times" (1 Peter 1:20). At the same time, Peter referred to the coming of Christ as a future event "ready to be revealed in the last time" (1 Peter 1:5). It is clear that he views the last times as both a present reality and a future event.

The Bible makes several things clear about the coming of Christ and the end of the age.

First, *we are living in the Last Days.* Every generation of Christians has lived with the hope of the imminent return of Christ. We believe that He could return at any moment. There is no prophetic event that *must* occur in order to open the way for Him to return. In fact, certain events, like the return of Israel to her land, indicate that we are closer to the end than ever before.

Second, *God's timetable is not our timetable.* Peter himself tells us that "in the last days scoffers will come," questioning the promise of His second coming (2 Peter 3:3-4). They will reject the idea of God's intervention in His creation, suggesting that all things are moving on at their own pace without God. They will also fail to anticipate the judgment of God which shall come upon the world in the future (2 Peter 3:7). In this context Peter reminds us: "With the Lord a day is like a thousand years, and a thousand years like a day" (2 Peter 3:8). God's perspective is not limited to human time. By God's timetable, Jesus has been back in heaven for less than two days! Don't mistake the patience of God for a change in His plans. He is waiting, giving us time to repent. The Bible warns: "He who is coming will come and will not delay" (Hebrews 10:37).

Third, *Christ's coming is closer than it has ever been.* The Bible emphatically promises that Christ is coming again (Luke 12:40; Philippians 3:20; Titus 2:13; Hebrews 9:28). The Scripture urges us to be watching, waiting, and ready for our Lord to return. Every day that passes brings us one day closer to His coming. Whether He returns next week or a thousand years from now, we are to be living as though He were coming today.

HOW SHOULD WE LIVE?

The hope of the Second Coming is the strongest reminder in Scripture to encourage us to live right until Jesus comes. The Apostle John said, "Continue in Him, so that when He appears we may be confident and unashamed before Him at His coming. . . . But we know that when He appears, we shall be like Him for we shall see Him as He is. Everyone who has this hope in Him purifies himself, just as He is pure" (1 John 2:28; 3:2-3).

The ultimate incentive to right living is the fact that we will face our Lord when He comes again. No matter what our failures and mistakes in the past, each of us needs to be ready when He comes. We may not be able to undo all the damage of our own doing in this life, but we have a promise of a better life tomorrow, when Jesus comes again.

First, *you need to know Jesus Christ personally.* The whole purpose of our Lord's first coming was to die as the atoning sacrifice for our sins. He came to pay the price for our sins so that we might be forgiven and released from the penalty of eternal death. He is called the Redeemer because He has redeemed us from God's judgment against our sin. Peter said: "You were redeemed . . . with the precious blood of Christ. . . . He was chosen before the Creation of the world, but was revealed in these last times for your sake. Through Him you believe in God, who raised Him from the dead and glorified Him, and so your faith and hope are in God" (1 Peter 1:18-21).

Second, *you need to commit your life to Him by faith.* Salvation is not something we can earn by our own good works, nor is it something we deserve. It must be received as a free gift from God. The Bible says, "Christ died for sins once for all, the righteous for the unrighteous, to bring you to God" (1 Peter 3:18). The Gospel ("good news") is the message that Christ died for our sins, was buried, and rose again (1 Corinthians 15:3-4). The invitation of the Gospel calls us to personal faith in those facts. The Bible says, "To all who received Him, to those who believed in His name, He gave the right to become the children of God" (John 1:12).

Third, *you need to surrender to His lordship.* Jesus Christ said that He came into the world to save sinners and call them to be His disciples. He further commissioned those disciples to go into the whole world and make more disciples, calling them to accountability to the lordship of Christ (Matthew 28:19-20). We are encouraged to be "clear minded and self-controlled" (1 Peter 4:7), so that we may serve the Lord Jesus faithfully.

THE ULTIMATE PRIORITY

There are many things that demand our attention in life. There are many voices calling to us and many images that flash across the screens of our minds. These have been difficult days. War is never an easy thing. It focuses our attention on the ultimate issues of life and death. It reminds us all of our own vulnerability.

Death is the great equalizer! It makes no difference how rich or poor, famous or infamous, respected or rejected you may have been in this life. When you face death you are facing an impartial judge. The Bible reminds us that "all have sinned" (Romans 3:23) and the "wages of sin is death" (Romans 6:23). When death comes knocking at your door, the only thing that really matters is that you are ready to face it.

"How can I be ready?" Tom asked me recently. "I know that I am running out of time." He had been fighting conviction and resisting God for a long time.

"You must respond by faith to God's promise to save you,"

I replied. "Christ died for your sins and rose from the dead to give you eternal life. Trusting Him for your salvation means believing that when He died, He died for you and that when He rose, He rose for you. The basic invitation of Scripture says: 'Everyone who calls on the name of the Lord will be saved' " (Romans 10:13).

"Have you ever asked Him to save you and believed that He would?" I asked.

"No, not really," he replied, as he dropped his head.

"Would you like to ask Him to forgive your sins, save your soul, and take you to heaven?" I asked further.

"Yes, I would!" he replied emphatically.

As we bowed our heads and prayed, he called upon the Lord Jesus Christ by faith to save Him and believed He did.

When we finished praying together, Tom looked at me and said, "Now, I'm ready because I believe He will keep His promise to me."

You can have that same kind of assurance in your life. You may have been drawn to an interest in prophecies of the end times in order to think through the question of your own future destiny. Perhaps all this talk of Armageddon, the coming of Christ, and the end of the age has made you realize that you are not ready to meet Him when He comes. Perhaps you have realized that the end could come at any moment and you are not prepared to step into eternity.

There is no better time to settle the question of your own eternal destiny than right now. John the Baptist called Jesus, "the Lamb of God, who takes away the sin of the world" (John 1:29). Won't you let Him take your sin away? Bow your heart, soul, mind, and head before Him and ask Him to save you right now.

When Billy Graham was asked, on a popular television show, to summarize what his life and ministry were all about, he simply quoted John 3:16, "For God so loved the world that

He gave His one and only Son, that whoever believes in Him shall not perish but have eternal life."

The clock of human history is ticking away the moments of time. It neither speeds up nor slows down. It just keeps on ticking continually and relentlessly, moving us closer and closer to the end of the age. How close we now are to the end will only be revealed by time itself. Don't gamble with your eternal destiny. Time may very well be running out. Make sure you are ready.

NOTES

CHAPTER ONE

1. Hal Lindsey is the author of the best-selling, *Late Great Planet Earth* (Grand Rapids: Zondervan, 1970) and a popular prophecy teacher.

2. Dave Hunt, *Global Peace and the Rise of the Antichrist* (Eugene, Ore.: Harvest House, 1990), p. 5.

3. Mikhail Gorbachev, "U.S.S.R. Arms Reduction," *Vital Speeches of the Day*, 1 Feb. 1989, p. 230. Delivered at the United Nations, New York, 7 Dec. 1988. Quoted by Hunt, *Global Peace*, p. 162.

4. Cf. Hunt, *Global Peace*, pp. 161–62.

5. Quoted by Tom Hayes, "Field of Conflict," New York Times News Service in the *St. Louis Post-Dispatch*, 5 Sept. 1990, sec. C, p. 1.

6. "What Comes Next?" in "War: Special Report," *Fortune*, 11 Feb. 1991, p. 36.

7. "The Fog of War," *Time*, 4 Feb. 1991, p. 18.

8. See the detailed description in C.H. Dyer, *The Rise of Babylon* (Wheaton, Ill.: Tyndale House, 1991).

9. "More Than a Madman," *Newsweek,* 7 Jan. 1991, pp. 20–21.

10. Ibid.

11. *Time,* 4 Feb. 1991, p. 18.

12. *Time,* 28 Jan. 1991, p. 29.

13. Ibid., p. 70.

14. Ibid., p. 65.

15. Ibid.

16. Hunt, *Global Peace,* p. 161.

17. John F. Walvoord, *Armageddon, Oil and the Middle East Crisis* (Grand Rapids: Zondervan, 1990), p. 18.

18. Quoted by E. Hindson, "The End is Near . . . Or Is It?" *World,* 24 Nov. 1990, p. 12.

19. See Paul Christianson, *Reformers and Babylon: English Apocalyptic Visions from the Reformation to the Eve of the Civil War* (Toronto: University of Toronto, 1978); K.R. Firth, *Apocalyptic Tradition in Reformation Britain 1530–1645* (Oxford: Oxford University, 1979); E. Hindson, *Puritan's Use of Scripture in the Development of an Apocalyptical Hermeneutic* (Pretoria: University of South Africa, 1984).

20. Harry Rimmer, *The Shadow of Coming Events* (Grand Rapids: Eerdmans, 1943).

CHAPTER TWO

1. This position is advocated by John Walvoord, *Armageddon, Oil and the Middle East Crisis* (Grand Rapids: Zondervan, 1990), pp. 129–35.

2. Ibid. p. 131.

3. See John Lamb, "Power to the People" in *1992 Now,* published by IBM Europe (March 1989), pp. 8–9; and "Reshaping

Europe: 1992 and Beyond," *Business Week*, 12 Dec. 1988, pp. 48–51.

4. "Freedom!" *Time*, 20 Nov. 1989, p. 26.

5. "Age of Anxiety," *Newsweek*, 31 Dec. 1990, p. 20.

6. "A Soviet Bombshell," *Newsweek*, 31 Dec. 1990, pp. 50–52.

7. "Turning Visions into Reality," *Time*, 11 Dec. 1989, p. 36.

8. Dave Hunt, *The Coming Peace* (Eugene, Ore.: Harvest House, 1990).

9. "Gorbachev, God and Socialism," *Time*, 11 Dec. 1989, p. 38.

10. See the helpful and insightful comments of David Jeremiah, *Escape the Coming Night* (Dallas: Word, 1990), pp. 167–81. He notes that the Great Prostitute of the end times has two faces: apostasy and religion.

11. One of the worst examples of excessive prophetic speculation is J.R. Church, *Hidden Prophecies in the Psalms* (Oklahoma City, Okla.: Prophecy Publications, 1986). He finds British General Allenby in Psalm 17 conquering Jerusalem in 1917; Psalms 39–44 tell the story of the Holocaust from 1939 to 1944; and Psalm 48 predicts the birth of Israel in 1948!

12. Cf. Ed Dobson and Ed Hindson, *The Seduction of Power* (Old Tappan, N.J.: Revell, 1988), "Armageddon Theology: Preaching Politics and the End of the World," pp. 77–92. Also, Ed Dobson and Ed Hindson, "Apocalypse Now? What Fundamentalists Believe About the End of the World," *Policy Review* (Fall 1986), pp. 16–22.

13. See Lorraine Boettner, *The Millennium* (Philadelphia: Presbyterian & Reformed, 1957); J.M. Kik, *An Eschatology of Victory* (Philadelphia: Presbyterian & Reformed, 1971); R.J. Rushdoony, *Thy Kingdom Come* (Fairfax, Va.: Chalcedon, 1975); David Chilton, *Paradise Restored* (Tyler, Texas: Do-

minion, 1984); J.J. Davis, *Christ's Victorious Kingdom* (Grand Rapids: Baker, 1986).

14. See J.E. Adams, *The Time Is at Hand* (Philadelphia: Presbyterian & Reformed, 1970); G.C. Berkouwer, *The Return of Christ* (Grand Rapids: Eerdmans, 1962); P.E. Hughes, *Interpreting Prophecy* (Grand Rapids: Eerdmans, 1976); and A. Hoekema, *The Bible and the Future* (Grand Rapids: Eerdmans, 1979).

15. See H.A. Hoyt, *The End Times* (Chicago: Moody, 1969); Rene Pache, *The Return of Jesus Christ* (Chicago: Moody, 1955); J.D. Pentecost, *Things to Come* (Grand Rapids: Zondervan, 1958); Tim LaHaye, *The Beginning of the End* (Wheaton, Ill.: Tyndale House, 1972); Leon Wood, *The Bible and Future Events* (Grand Rapids: Zondervan, 1973).

16. Cf. Allen Beechick, *The Pre-Tribulation Rapture* (Denver: Accent, 1980); Guy Duty, *Escape from the Coming Tribulation* (Minneapolis: Bethany Fellowship, 1975); J. Walvoord, *The Blessed Hope and the Tribulation* (Grand Rapids: Zondervan, 1975); G.E. Ladd, *The Blessed Hope* (Grand Rapids: Eerdmans, 1956; R.H. Gundry, *The Church and the Tribulation* (Grand Rapids: Zondervan, 1973); H. Lindsell, *The Gathering Storm* (Wheaton, Ill.: Tyndale House, 1980); M.J. Erickson, *Contemporary Options in Eschatology* (Grand Rapids: Baker, 1977).

17. David Jeremiah, *Escape the Coming Night*, p. 85.

18. Comments during the Reagan vs. Mondale Presidential debates in 1984, as commonly reported in the press.

19. See Dobson and Hindson, *The Seduction of Power*, p. 90ff. for details.

20. Frank Peretti, *This Present Darkness* (Westchester, Ill.: Crossway, 1986), emphasizes this in a graphic form in his best-selling novel.

21. Alexander Solzhenitsyn, *Warning to the West* (New York: Farrar, Straus, and Giroux, 1976), p. 145.

CHAPTER 3

1. John Walvoord, *Matthew: Thy Kingdom Come* (Chicago: Moody, 1974), p. 181. Cf. also E. Hindson, "Matthew," in *Liberty Study Bible*, ed. E. Hindson and W. Kroll (Nashville: Thomas Nelson, 1983), pp. 1946–52.

2. Cf. Homer Kent, Jr., "Matthew," in *Wycliffe Bible Commentary* (Chicago: Moody, 1962), p. 85ff.

3. William S. LaSor, *The Truth About Armageddon* (Grand Rapids: Baker, 1982), p. 15.

4. J.P. Lange, *Commentary on the Holy Scriptures: Matthew* (Grand Rapids: Zondervan, n.d.), p. 428.

5. W.F. Arndt and F.W. Gingrich, *A Greek-English Lexicon of the New Testament* (Chicago: University of Chicago, 1957), p. 153.

6. Kent, "Matthew," p. 89.

7. LaSor, *The Truth About Armageddon*, p. 122.

8. See Amos 5:18-20; Joel 1:15; 2:1, 11, 31; Isaiah 2:11-19; 13:6-9; 22:5; 34:8; Jeremiah 46:10; Zephaniah 1:7-8; Ezekiel 7:10; 13:5; 30:3; and Zechariah 14:1.

9. Charles Dyer, *The Rise of Babylon* (Wheaton, Ill.: Tyndale House, 1991) makes a great deal out of Hussein's attempt to refurnish the excavated ruins of Ancient Babylon as if this were a fulfillment of prophecy. Yet the *Washington Post* (10 Feb. 1975, sec. A, p. 5) reported that an Italian archeologist had been employed by the pre-Hussein government of Iraq to rebuild the Tower of Babel over fifteen years ago.

CHAPTER 4

1. Edgar C. Whisenant, *88 Reasons Why the Rapture Will Be in 1988* (Nashville: World Bible Society, 1988).

2. See E. Hindson, *Introduction to Puritan Theology* (Grand Rapids: Baker, 1976); P.E. Hughes, *Theology of the English Reformers* (Grand Rapids: Eerdmans, 1965).

3. This is examined at great length and detail in Paul Christianson, *Reformers and Babylon* (Toronto: University of Toronto, 1978); K.R. Firth, *The Apocalyptic Traditions in Reformation Britain* (Oxford: Oxford University, 1979); E. Hindson, *The Puritan's Use of Scripture in the Development of an Apocalyptical Hermeneutic* (Pretoria: University of South Africa, 1984); W. Haller, *Foxe's "Book of Martyrs" and the Elect Nation* (New York: Harper & Row, 1963); Christopher Hill, *Antichrist in Seventeenth-Century England* (London: Oxford University, 1971); Tai Liu, *Discord in Zion: The Puritan Divines and the Puritan Revolution 1640-1660* (The Hague: Martinus Nijhoff, 1973).

4. See S. Ozment, *The Age of Reform 1250-1550: An Intellectual and Religious History of Late Medieval and Reformation Europe* (New Haven: Yale University, 1980), pp. 103-15; and M. Reeves, *The Influence of Prophecy in the Later Middle Ages: A Study of Joachimism* (Oxford: Clarendon, 1969).

5. Wyclif, *Select English Writings* (Oxford: Oxford University, 1929), pp. 66-74.

6. See details in Firth, *Apocalyptic Traditions in Reformation Britain*, pp. 11-15; J.M. Headley, *Luther's View of Church History* (New Haven: Yale University, 1963), pp. 242-46; M. Reeves, *Influence of Prophecy in the Later Middle Ages*, pp. 233-35.

7. John Calvin, *Commentary on Romans and Thessalonians*, Trans. R. Mackenzie, in Calvin's Commentaries, ed. Torrance & Torrance (Grand Rapids: Eerdmans, 1959-1972), vol. 4,

pp. 396–99; and *The First Epistle of John*, trans. T.H.L. Parker, vol. 3, p. 256.

8. John Bale, "The Image of Both Churches"; in *Select Works of Bishop Bale* (London: Parker Society, 1849) and "A Comedy Concerning Three Laws," in J.S. Farmer, ed., *The Dramatic Writings of John Bale, Bishop of Ossory* (London: Early English Drama Society, 1907). Cf. also J. Harris, *John Bale: A Study in the Minor Literature of the Reformation* (Urbana: University of Illinois, 1940); H. McCusker, *John Bale: Dramatist and Antiquary* (Bryn Mawr: Haverford College, 1952); and Firth, *Apocalyptic Traditions*, pp. 32–68.

9. Walter Raleigh, *History of the World* in *The Works of Sir Walter Raleigh* (Oxford: Oxford University, 1829), Book 1, chap. 8, sec. 4, vol. 2, pp. 261–65; Book 5, chap. 6, sec. 12, vol. 1, pp. 898–900.

10. Hugh Broughton, *A Revelation of the Apocalypse* (Amsterdam: 1610), pp. 137–250. Cf. comments by Firth, *Apocalyptic Traditions*, pp. 152–63 and Christianson, *Reformers and Babylon*, pp. 107–11. The latter remarked of Broughton's date, "He could still be right!" (p. 109)

11. John Napier, *A Plaine Discovery of the Whole Revelation of St. John* (Edinburgh: 1593 and London: 1611). Cf. also R. Clouse, "John Napier and Apocalyptic Thought," *Sixteenth Century Journal*, V, (1974), pp. 101–14.

12. His writings are collected in *The Works of Thomas Brightman* (London: 1644). Cf. also R. Clouse, "The Apocalyptic Interpretation of Thomas Brightman and Joseph Mede," *Bulletin of the Evangelical Theological Society*, XI (1968), pp. 181–93.

13. Joseph Mede, *The Key of the Revelation* (London: 1643). The Latin edition appeared in 1627. Cf. also his *The Apostasy of the Latter Times* (London: 1642). On the significance of Mede's views, see Peter Toon, *Puritans, the Millennium and the Future of Israel* (London: James Clarke, 1970), pp. 42–56.

14. *A Glimpse of Sion's Glory* (London: 1641) and *A Sermon to the Fifth Monarchy* (London: 1654). Cf. also Toon, *Puritans,* pp. 64–65 and Appendix I.

15. John Owen, "Righteous Zeal Encouraged by Divine Protection" (31 Jan. 1649), in *Works of John Owen* (London: W.H. Goold, 1850–1853), vol. 8, pp. 128ff.

16. See the excellent discussion in Charles Ryrie, *Dispensationalism Today* (Chicago: Moody, 1965), pp. 71–75.

17. See Clarence Bass, *Backgrounds to Dispensationalism* (Grand Rapids: Eerdmans, 1960), pp. 64–99.

18. *The Collected Writings of J.N. Darby* (London: Morrish, 1867), vol. 2, pp. 568–73.

19. The history of this period is well documented by Timothy Weber, *Living in the Shadow of the Second Coming: American Premillennialism 1875-1925* (New York: Oxford University, 1979).

20. This is the scheme generally followed in the *Scofield Reference Bible* (New York: Oxford University, 1909) and slightly modified in the *New Scofield Reference Bible* (1967).

21. For a thorough account of the history, beliefs, and practices of Mormons, Adventists, and Jehovah's Witnesses, see Anthony Hoekema, *The Four Major Cults* (Grand Rapids: Zondervan, 1963).

22. See the excellent analysis of this by Stanley N. Gundry, "Hermeneutics or *Zeitgeist* as the Determining Factor in the History of Eschatologies?" *Journal of the Evangelical Theological Society,* 20:1 (1977), p. 50ff.

23. Daniel R. Mitchell, "Is the Rapture on Schedule?" *Fundamentalist Journal* (Oct. 1988), p. 66.

CHAPTER 5

1. Commonly reported in the news media on Feb. 8, 1991.

2. Quoted by John Phillips, *Only God Can Prophesy!* (Wheaton, Ill.: Harold Shaw, 1975), p. 27.

3. Arthur Levine, *When Dreams and Heroes Died: A Portrait of Today's College Student* (San Francisco: Jossey-Bass, 1980). Cf. also Alan Bloom, *The Closing of the American Mind* (New York: Simon & Schuster, 1986).

4. See Phillips, *Only God Can Prophesy!* pp. 105–7.

5. Ibid., pp. 111–12.

6. "A War Against the Earth," *Time,* 4 Feb. 1991, pp. 32–33.

7. Dave Hunt, *Global Peace and the Rise of the Antichrist* (Eugene, Ore.: Harvest House, 1990), p. 163.

8. "Playing With Fire," *Time,* 18 Sept. 1989, pp. 76–80.

9. *Europe* (Nov. 1989), p. 20ff.

10. "Europe Starts Federation Process," *St. Louis Post-Dispatch,* 12 Nov. 1990, sec. A, p. 3.

11. Steve Ludwig, "Electronic Money Will Change Your Life," *Sky,* Jan. 1974, pp. 19–21.

12. Dave Hunt, *Global Peace,* p. 220.

13. Ibid., p. 223.

14. The identification of these names has been verified by extensive archeological research and is to be preferred over identifications often given in popular books on prophecy. For a detailed examination of the evidence, see E.M. Yamauchi, *Foes From the Northern Frontier* (Grand Rapids: Baker, 1982). Cf. also E.D. Phillips, "The Scythian Domination in Western Asia: Its Record in History, Scripture and Archaeology," *World Archaeology* (1972), p. 129ff.

15. John Walvoord, *Armageddon, Oil and the Middle East Crisis* (Grand Rapids: Zondervan, 1990), pp. 137–47.

16. Yamauchi, *Foes From the Northern Frontier*, pp. 29–36, 63–68.

17. Charles Dyer, *The Rise of Babylon* (Wheaton, Ill.: Tyndale House, 1991), pp. 161–204.

18. Gleason Archer, "Isaiah," *Wycliffe Bible Commentary* (Chicago: Moody, 1962), p. 621. Cf. also E. Hindson, "Isaiah," *Liberty Bible Commentary* (Nashville: Thomas Nelson, 1983), p. 1322ff.

19. For an excellent history of ancient Babylon, see Joan Oates, *Babylon* (London: Thomas & Hudson, 1979); H.W.F. Saggs, *The Greatness That Was Babylon* (New York: Macmillan, 1962); and E. Yamauchi, "Babylon," in R.K. Harrison, ed., *Major Cities of the Biblical World* (Nashville: Thomas Nelson, 1985), pp. 32–48.

20. Oates, *Babylon*, pp. 139–43.

21. Ibid., p. 143.

22. Dyer, *Rise of Babylon*, p. 192.

23. Ibid., p. 190.

24. Isaiah delivered oracles against Babylon (13:1), Assyria (14:25), Philistia (14:29), Moab (15:1), Damascus (17:1), Cush (18:1), Egypt (19:1), the Desert (21:1), Edom (21:11), Arabia (21:13), and Tyre (23:1).

25. W.A. VanGemeren, "Isaiah," in W. Elwell, ed., *Evangelical Commentary on the Bible* (Grand Rapids: Baker, 1989), p. 484.

CHAPTER 6

1. John Naisbitt and Patricia Aburdene, *Megatrends 2000* (New York: William Morrow, 1990).

2. Dave Hunt, *Global Peace and the Rise of the Antichrist* (Eugene, Ore.: Harvest House, 1990), p. 55.

3. *Time,* 11 Dec. 1989, p. 37.

4. Hunt, *Global Peace,* pp. 60–61.

5. *Time,* 7 Jan. 1991, p. 23.

6. Commonly televised Jan. 16, 1991, and reported in the press, Jan. 17, 1991.

7. George Will, "Europe's Second Reformation," *Newsweek,* 20 Nov. 1989, p. 90.

8. "Charging Ahead," *Time,* 18 Sept. 1989, pp. 40–45.

9. Ibid., p. 43.

10. *U.S. News & World Report,* 15 Oct. 1990, p. 64.

11. Naisbitt and Aburdene, *Megatrends 2000,* pp. 49–50.

12. Eric Salama, "Europe's New Shop Window," in *1992 Now,* published by IBM Europe, March 1989, p. 5.

13. Nicholas Colchester, "Freeing the Frontiers," *1992 Now,* p. 6.

14. John Lamb, "Power to the People," *1992 Now,* pp. 8–9.

15. Ibid., p. 9.

16. Hunt, *Global Peace,* p. 73.

CHAPTER 7

1. Abraham—Genesis 12:1-3, 7; 15; 17:1-14; 18:18-19; 22:15-18. Isaac—Genesis 26:2-5. Jacob—Genesis 28:12-15.

2. See Dave Hunt, *Global Peace and the Rise of the Antichrist* (Eugene, Ore.: Harvest House, 1990).

3. Nicholas deLange, *Atlas of the Jewish World* (New York: Facts on File, 1984), pp. 38–41. He cites large Jewish populations at

Baghdad, Cairo, Ghazna, and Samarkand during the Middle Ages.

4. Abba Eban, *My People: The Story of the Jews* (New York: Random House, 1968), p. 151. See also, A.W. Kac, *The Rebirth of the State of Israel* (Grand Rapids: Baker, 1958).

5. John Phillips, *Only God Can Prophesy!* (Wheaton, Ill.: Harold Shaw, 1975), p. 61.

6. John Walvoord, *Armageddon, Oil and the Middle East Crisis* (Grand Rapids: Zondervan, 1990), pp. 49–51.

7. Ibid., p. 129.

CHAPTER 8

1. Quotation from the Christic Institute in E. Dobson and E. Hindson, "Apocalypse Now? What Fundamentalists Believe About the End of the World," in *Policy Review* (Fall 1986), pp. 16–22.

2. For a detailed study, see Herman Hoyt, *The End Times* (Chicago: Moody, 1969), pp. 9–10, 63–65.

3. See the excellent discussions of J.D. Pentecost, *Things to Come* (Grand Rapids: Zondervan, 1964), pp. 239–50; and Alva McClain, *Daniel's Prophecy of the Seventy Weeks* (Grand Rapids: Zondervan, 1940).

4. Robert Anderson, *The Coming Prince* (London: Hodder & Stoughten, 1909).

5. Cf. Elias Bickerman, *From Ezra to the Last of the Maccabees* (New York: Schoken, 1966); D.S. Russell, *Between the Testaments* (London: SCM Press, 1960); John Rogerson, *Atlas of the Bible* (New York: Facts on File, 1985), pp. 36–39.

6. See "Temple, Herod's," in *Eerdmans Bible Dictionary* (Grand Rapids: Eerdmans, 1987), pp. 991–92; T. Cornell and J.

Matthews, *Atlas of the Roman World* (New York: Facts on File, 1982), pp. 79–81, 162–64.

7. See "Diaspora of the Jews," in W.A. Elwell, ed., *Baker Encyclopedia of the Bible* (Grand Rapids: Baker, 1988), vol. 1, pp. 623–25; Nicholas de Lange, *Atlas of the Jewish World* (New York: Facts on File, 1984), pp. 46–53.

8. See Revelation 5:6-14; 14:1-5; 19:19; 21:9, 22-23; 22:1-3.

CHAPTER 9

1. These thoughts are developed from E. Dobson and E. Hindson, *The Seduction of Power* (Old Tappan, N.J.: Revell, 1988), pp. 93–109.

2. Paul Johnson, *Modern Times: The World from the Twenties to the Eighties* (San Francisco: Harper & Row, 1983).

3. Charles Colson, *Against the Night* (Ann Arbor: Servant, 1989), p. 19.

4. For an excellent assessment of these ideas, cf. Donald Bloesch, *Crumbling Foundations* (Grand Rapids: Zondervan, 1984); Harvey Cox, *Religion in the Secular City* (New York: Simon & Schuster, 1984); Carl F.H. Henry, *The Christian Mindset in a Secular Society* (Portland: Multnomah Press, 1984); Tim LaHaye, *The Race for the 21st Century* (Nashville: Thomas Nelson, 1986); Richard Neuhaus, *The Naked Public Square* (Grand Rapids: Eerdmans, 1984); R.C. Sproul, *Lifeviews: Understanding the Ideas That Shape Society* (Old Tappan, N.J.: Revell, 1986); and Cal Thomas, *The Death of Ethics in America* (Waco, Texas: Word, 1988).

5. Allan Bloom, *The Closing of the American Mind* (New York: Simon & Schuster, 1987). The author argues that higher education has been hijacked by a system of philosophy which has impoverished the souls of today's students.

6. Ibid., p. 34.

7. Arthur Levine, *When Dreams and Heroes Died: A Portrait of Today's College Student* (San Francisco: Jossey-Bass, 1980). Levine's study, sponsored by the Carnegie Foundation for the Advancement of Teaching, found that today's students are self-centered "escapists" who want little responsibility for solving society's problems.

8. See Karen Hoyt, *The New Age Rage* (Old Tappan, N.J.: Revell, 1987) and Elliot Miller, *A Crash Course on the New Age Movement* (Grand Rapids: Baker, 1989).

9. Francis Schaeffer, *Escape from Reason* (Chicago: InterVarsity, 1965).

10. Rene Pache, *The Return of Jesus Christ* (Chicago: Moody, 1955) p. 109.

11. See Allen Beechick, *The Pre-Tribulation Rapture* (Denver: Accent, 1980); Guy Duty, *Escape from the Coming Tribulation* (Minneapolis: Bethany Fellowship, 1975); John Walvoord, *The Blessed Hope and the Tribulation* (Grand Rapids: Zondervan, 1975).

12. See J.O. Buswell, *A Systematic Theology of the Christian Religion* (Grand Rapids: Zondervan, 1962), vol. 2, pp. 393–450; N.B. Harrison, *The End* (Minneapolis: Harrison, 1941); M. Rosenthal, *The Pre-Wrath Rapture* (Nashville: Thomas Nelson, 1990).

13. See G.E. Ladd, *The Blessed Hope* (Grand Rapids: Eerdmans, 1956); R.H. Gundry, *The Church and the Tribulation* (Grand Rapids: Zondervan, 1973).

CHAPTER 10

1. The interpretation of Isaiah's "Little Apocalypse" (Isaiah 24) hinges on the translation of the Hebrew word 'erets. The KJV translates it "earth" six times and "land" three times, whereas the RSV and NIV translate it "earth" each time. The interpretation revolves around whether the judgments described here

refer to the whole earth or just the land of Israel. In verse 4, *'erets* is used in parallel with *tebel,* the Hebrew word for "world." Edward Young, *The Book of Isaiah* (Grand Rapids: Eerdmans, 1965), vol. 2, p. 154, quotes Kittel in asserting that *tebel* is never restricted to the land of Judah. There can be then no doubt that Isaiah has the whole world in view in this prophecy.

2. See E. Hindson, "Isaiah," in E. Hindson and W. Kroll, eds., *Liberty Bible Commentary* (Nashville: Thomas Nelson, 1983), pp. 1335–38; 1350–51; and Gleason Archer, "Isaiah," *Wycliffe Bible Commentary* (Chicago: Moody, 1962), p. 633.

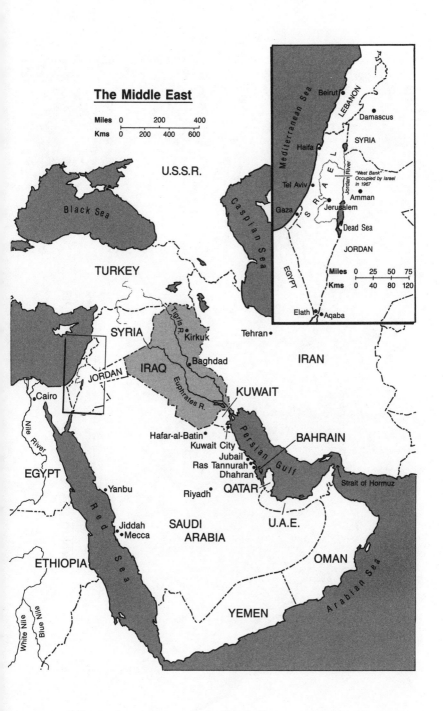

The Middle East

Miles 0   200   400
Kms 0   200   400   600

U.S.S.R.

Black Sea

Caspian Sea

TURKEY

Mediterranean Sea

Beirut
LEBANON
Damascus
SYRIA
Haifa
Jordan River
Tel Aviv
"West Bank" Occupied by Israel in 1967
Gaza
Jerusalem
Amman
I S R A E L
Dead Sea
JORDAN
EGYPT

Miles 0   25   50   75
Kms 0   40   80   120

Elath   Aqaba

SYRIA

Tigris R.
Kirkuk
Tehran

Baghdad

JORDAN
IRAQ
Euphrates R.

IRAN

Cairo

KUWAIT

Hafar-al-Batin
Kuwait City
Jubail
Ras Tannurah
Dhahran
QATAR

Persian Gulf

BAHRAIN

Strait of Hormuz

EGYPT

Nile River

Yanbu

Riyadh

U.A.E.

SAUDI
ARABIA

Jiddah
Mecca

Red Sea

ETHIOPIA

OMAN

Arabian Sea

White Nile
Blue Nile

YEMEN

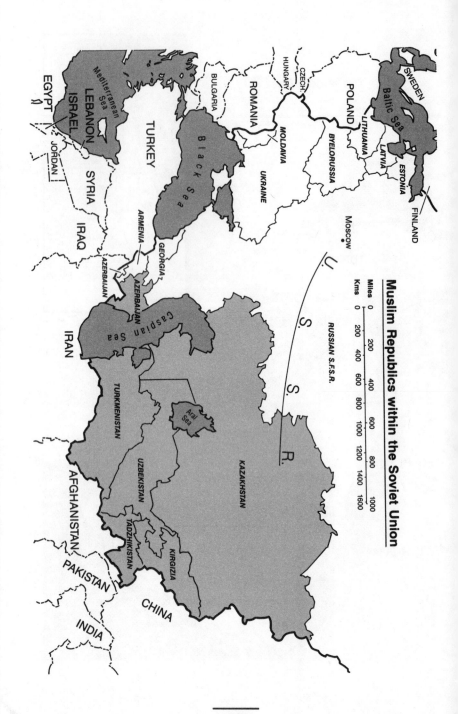

Muslim Republics within the Soviet Union

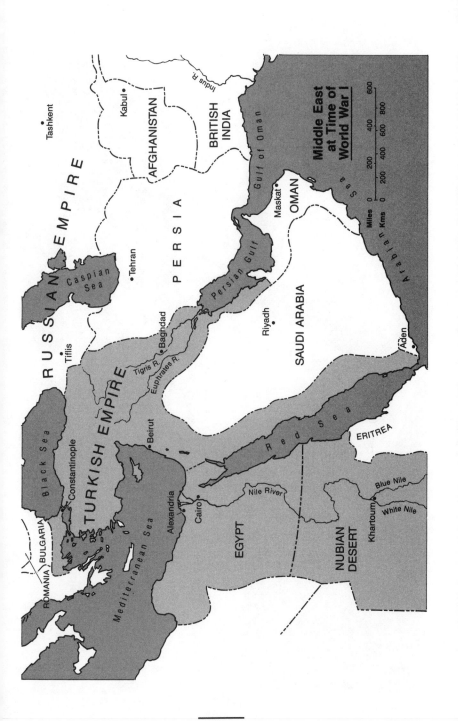

Middle East
at Time of
World War I

RUSSIAN EMPIRE

Tashkent

AFGHANISTAN

Kabul

BRITISH
INDIA

Indus R.

PERSIA

Gulf of Oman

Maskat

OMAN

Tehran

Caspian
Sea

Tiflis

Persian Gulf

Baghdad

Riyadh

SAUDI ARABIA

Arabian Sea

Aden

TURKISH EMPIRE

Tigris R.

Euphrates R.

Beirut

Black Sea

Constantinople

Red Sea

ERITREA

BULGARIA

Nile River

Blue Nile

ROMANIA

Alexandria

Cairo

Khartoum

White Nile

Mediterranean Sea

EGYPT

NUBIAN
DESERT

Miles   0   200   400   600
Kms   0   200   400   600   800

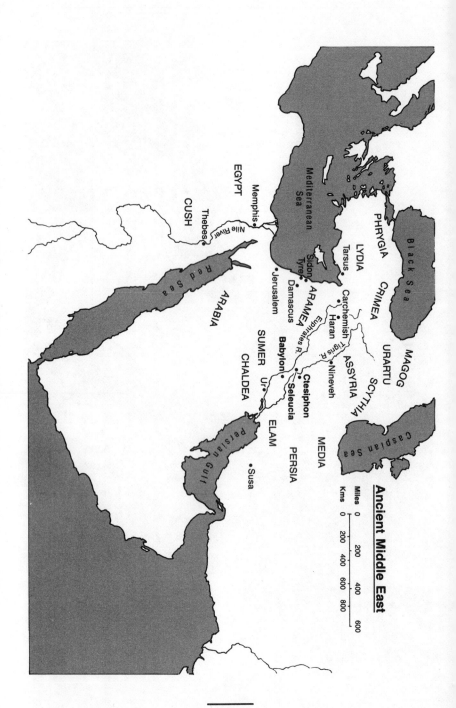

Ancient Middle East

Miles 0   200   400   600

Kms 0   200   400   600   800

EGYPT

CUSH

Memphis

Thebes

Nile River

Red Sea

ARABIA

Mediterranean Sea

Jerusalem

Sidon

Tyre

Damascus

ARAMEA

PHRYGIA

LYDIA

Tarsus

CRIMEA

Black Sea

MAGOG

URARTU

SCYTHIA

Carchemish

Haran

Euphrates R.

Tigris R.

Nineveh

ASSYRIA

SUMER

Babylon

Ur

CHALDEA

Ctesiphon

Seleucia

ELAM

MEDIA

PERSIA

Susa

Persian Gulf

Caspian Sea